Dear Anxiety, Let's Break Up

40 DEVOTIONS TO CONQUER WORRY AND FEAR

Amanda Porter, Ph.D

BroadStreet
PUBLISHING

BroadStreet Publishing® Group, LLC
Savage, Minnesota, USA
BroadStreetPublishing.com

Dear Anxiety, Let's Break Up: 40 Devotions to Conquer Worry and Fear
Copyright © 2021 Amanda Porter

978-1-4245-6254-1 (hardcover)
978-1-4245-6255-8 (e-book)

Stock or custom editions of BroadStreet Publishing titles may be purchased in bulk for educational, business, ministry, fundraising, or sales promotional use. For information, please email orders@broadstreetpublishing.com.

Design and typesetting | garborgdesign.com

Printed in China

21 22 23 24 25 5 4 3 2 1

Dedication

I'm still trying to find the line between professional
expert (of which I am) and authentic human being
who struggles (of which I also am).
To all my patients who allow me to be both.

Contents

Gentle Disclaimer

While I am a mental health professional, I recognize that I am not your provider and do not know the details of your personal experience with anxiety. I hope you find comfort in the words I've written within these pages, and I recommend that you discuss the teachings with your personal medical provider, who knows you best. The stories and names of patients in this book have been altered to protect their identities. These stories are intended to serve as reflections and applications to help those who struggle with anxiety. You are not alone. We are in this together.

Introduction

I don't know about you, but I've seen countless hardcover gift books and devotionals embossed and flowered with swirling cursive, posing on the shelves of Christian bookstores (before most of them closed their doors). These books contain lovely language that seems convincing in the form of promise and posture. They tout the vast promises of God in tones that tell me I am deserving and entitled to every good thing that comes to me, as if everything is rainbows and butterflies simply because I've turned my life over in service to my Savior.

We've been misled, whether by our own unreasonable expectations and assumptions or by external influences, including these devotionals and gift books that guarantee peace from worry and anxiety solely because God loves us and wants what's best for us. While it is important to remember the riches that we will inherit as a result of our love and faithfulness in Christ, it's also important that we read the Bible and understand its context. This is particularly important when we examine the Scriptures for instruction on how to deal with our anxieties.

This devotional may be different from others you've read. I want to offer not only encouragement but also education. I'm not interested in a shallow glossing-over of what Scripture has to say about dealing with emotions. While I do want to offer comfort and direction, my job here is not to give you a warm and fuzzy feeling. Our relationship with God is not a transactional one, and I don't want you fooled into believing that a life lived in service to God is supposed to be a life without stumble, flounder, and waver.

Anxiety is a tricky business. As a scientist and clinician, I understand what anxiety is, does, and communicates. I can easily rattle off what a successful treatment plan should entail for someone who is struggling with anxiety. As a human being, I admit that my own anxieties (both generalized and social) dupe me. A better way to face our worries exists, friend, and it's rooted in our faith. Our faith can overcome our fear. It is possible to pivot from living a life of fear to living a life of faith.

Perhaps you wonder if anxiety is a sin or if it's okay to take medication to help with it. Maybe you're experiencing shame, guilt, or accusations that your faith in Christ should be enough to heal you. Maybe you're looking for actionable skills to help combat your anxiety with faith, or perhaps you want to learn more about it so that you can support a loved one who struggles with it. If any of those lines resonated with you, then please know that I wrote this book for you.

What do I mean when I use the word *anxiety*? Anxiety is feeling worried, nervous, or fearful. Anxious people feel a sense of dread or worry about a future outcome, and they may feel as if they have no control. More than that, anxiety is also a physical experience. Symptoms include headaches, muscle tension, shaky hands, and an upset stomach. Our heart rate increases, and our chest tightens. We may feel nauseated or weak, and it becomes difficult to breathe. We sweat and shake. And worse yet, other people may notice our physical responses, leading to feelings of shame and embarrassment.

Spiritual symptoms and implications are also commonly experienced with anxiety: a loss of meaning in life, a lack of hope for the future, or an inability to focus on God or meditate. I once had a patient describe their anxiety to me this way: "It's like having three hundred different web browser tabs open at once, all with information demanding my immediate attention, and I can't figure out which one to look at first." It's uncomfortable to say the very least.

At some point or another, we all feel anxiety. A life free of anxiety is simply not a thing that exists. But it's the presence of excessive, over-the-top, all-consuming anxiety or worry that warrants its classification as a disorder. Here's the textbook definition of Generalized Anxiety Disorder (GAD), which is the most common anxiety disorder that affects about forty million Americans (myself included), and one in ten people in the United Kingdom:

- One aspect is the presence of excessive anxiety or worry that is difficult to control for at least the past six months.

- At least three somatic (or physical) symptoms must also be present: among them restlessness or feeling keyed up, palpitations or increased heart rate, hyperventilation or difficulty catching your breath, being easily fatigued, difficulty concentrating, irritability, muscle tension, nausea or diarrhea, or sleep disturbance.[1]

I also classify anxiety as an *emotion* (not a sin, which we'll discuss later). We have emotions. It's the way our wiring works as humans, and these emotions are meant to be explored, not stuffed down or ignored. It's important to recognize and label our emotions so that we can master them instead of falling prey to emotion-driven behaviors we might later regret. Emotions communicate something, and sometimes they hear the message incorrectly. That's why our emotions get a seat at the metaphorical table, but they don't get to sit at the head of it.

Let's expand our scope and discuss mental health as a whole. Mental health is not merely the absence of disorders or diseases, and the World Health Organization defines it as "a state of well-being in which every individual realizes his or her own potential, can cope with the normal stresses of life, can work productively and fruitfully, and is able to make a contribution to her or his community."[2] Notice that mental health or wellness goes beyond the *absence* of illness. To be mentally well requires more than simply getting by. To be mentally well means that we are thriving and realizing our full potential. To be mentally well also means that we are productively contributing to our community, rippling out the blessings of our lives, and serving others. Our life goal as Jesus followers significantly overlaps with this definition of mental wellness.

The frustrating reality is that there is no gold standard or objective assessment when it comes to mental health diagnoses. It's a matter of interview and observation, meaning you sit and talk with a clinician who gets to know you and then diagnoses you. This means that a diagnosis has the potential to differ depending on the provider with whom you are working. I suspect that this lack of objectivity is where the unfortunate stigma surrounding mental health issues is born. The general public might conclude that without an objective assessment that delivers a clear, black-or-white diagnosis, all mental health diagnoses are unreliable, illegitimate, or less credible. This deeply saddens me.

Our biological stress response is natural and innate, and although it was God's design, it doesn't mean that it can't be overwhelming or all-consuming at times. Naturally, we seek relief. And as Jesus followers, we turn to Scripture for guidance. I personally have scoured the Bible for answers, direction, comfort, and encouragement. But I first went about it the wrong way. I found verses that told me I was beloved, adored, cherished, and protected by God. I expected immediate, long-lasting relief from my distress. I expected healing that didn't necessarily require effort from me apart from quick prayers to God. I expected neat, tidy circumstances with predictable, orderly outcomes. I didn't expect heartbreak, distress, and hassle. I didn't expect disappointment. I felt a huge disconnect between what I read in Scripture and what I was experiencing. I didn't feel protected from my anxieties; I felt alone and weighed down. I also felt bait-and-switched. To use a churchy word, I felt *forsaken*.

I want to save you some of the struggle I experienced, friend. I write these words for you, but I write them for myself too. While I have found a way to manage my day-to-day anxiety, I still feel a tug of war between calm and fear every day. I want you to understand that as you comb through Scripture on your own journey to peace, you, too, may feel disenchanted. That is, until you arrive at this glorious conclusion: On the front end of any struggle, the desired outcome is the absence of anxiety. But on the back end of victory, wisdom and nearness to God are most satisfying.

In this devotional, we will encounter verses, many from Psalms and Proverbs, that address how to cope with anxiety and combat fear with faith. However, parts of Scripture and many Proverbs are general rules, not promises or guarantees. Remember, friend, nowhere in Scripture are we promised comfort. In fact, the Bible promises the opposite: trial, discomfort, distress, and hardship. As 1 Peter 4:12 reads: "Dear friends, your faith is going to be tested as if it were going through fire. Do not be surprised at this" (NLV). As we read through Scripture in search of relief for our most anxious thoughts, we must analyze for ourselves whether each passage is descriptive or prescriptive and ask ourselves, *Is this a place where Scripture is informational or instructional? How does this particular passage apply to me in my personal recovery from anxiety?*

Everyone who reads this book will be at a different stage in their faith and in their battle with anxiety. Maybe you've been a Christian all your life, in which case I hope you are able to read the passages we cover with fresh eyes. Perhaps you are beginning your faith wanderings, and you want to understand what assurances lie in a man called Jesus. Maybe you are drowning in information but desperately searching for real direction.

I'll take you through the coping skills and reframing techniques rooted in Scripture that have been most helpful to me in my battle with anxiety. Within each day's entry you can expect to read a main verse, a brief anecdote or educational lesson, a takeaway message, a journaling prompt, and a closing prayer. At the end of each ten-day stretch, we will have a quarterly check-in. I understand that most of us lead busy lives, so it's difficult to find free time. I intentionally created this book so that it can be read in bite-sized pieces. Come and go as you need. You are always welcome.

To make the most of your encounter with this devotional, I recommend that you find a quiet, calm, and peaceful environment with minimal distractions in which to read. Cut out as much background noise as possible. Tranquil surroundings are impactful. Outer order brings forth inner calm. Perhaps even have a hot, yummy beverage close by.

Lastly, it's important to acknowledge and understand that we all cope differently, so everyone will likely walk away from this devotional with something different. Whether it's a complete lightbulb moment or simply reinforcement of a familiar concept, I consider any helpful takeaway a success.

Anxiety still whispers in my ear every day; she doesn't want me to forget her lies. However, I have found a great deal of comfort in God's Word when it comes to how I should approach my anxious way of thinking. Once you've finished working through this devotional, my hope is that you'll be able to say the same thing; that you, too, have been able to exchange overwhelming fear for soulful, lasting peace.

Cheering you on in recovery, wellness, and hope,

Amanda

Managing Emotions

He alone is my safe place. His wraparound presence always protects me as my champion defender. There's no risk of failure with God! So why would I let worry paralyze me, even when troubles multiply around me?

PSALM 62:6 TPT

How many emotions do you experience on a daily basis? Personally, I experience the full range. We all do. As humans, we are wired to experience emotions such as irritability, happiness, sadness, joy, weariness, anger, and anxiety. Some of these emotions are more comfortable than others, and some are easier to control. Which emotions do you struggle to manage the most? Do any of these emotions seem to rule your life? You can't see me raising my hand right now, but I struggle most with feelings of anxiety.

Anxiety can be a difficult experience to describe. I would define it as fear, worry, dread, or unease. Above all else, anxiety is an emotion. What's the definition of *emotion*? I've come across a few, and I like this one from the *American Heritage Science Dictionary* best: "A psychological state that arises spontaneously rather than through conscious effort and is sometimes accompanied by physiological changes; a feeling." After reading this definition, while wearing my scientist hat, this is what I know about emotions:

- Since each human being is unique, emotions are subjective.

- Since human beings are wired with an autonomic nervous system, emotions are spontaneous.

- Since we have nerves all over our body, emotions are physical.

- Since emotions do not come from time spent in conscious reasoning, emotions are not always rational.

I would invite you to read through this list again but substitute the word *anxiety* for *emotions*. *Anxiety* is subjective and spontaneous. *Anxiety* can be physical. *Anxiety* is not always rational. All of this means that anxiety is neither your fault nor a sin; it's an emotion. And since you are a human being, you are wired to experience emotions—including anxiety. However, it *is* your responsibility to learn how to manage your anxiety. In fact, one of the most vital skills a human being can learn is to manage his or her emotions. Learning to manage emotions does not come easily. It takes a lot of hard work, and like most things in life, comfort and change cannot coexist.

This is what I am learning: God loves me so much that he created me to be an intricate, individual, astoundingly complex person—emotions and all. He didn't make a mistake when he gave me these pounding emotions that often lead to racing thoughts and spiraling. I am sometimes overwhelmed by my anxiety, but that does not mean that I'm unfixable. God knew I would find a way to conquer my anxiety and then equipped me to share it with you so that you, too, can find success in your journey. And you will.

Emotions are communicators. In time and with practice, my emotions will hold no power over me.

Journaling Prompt

What is one example of when I managed my emotions well? What is one example of when my emotions overwhelmed me? What triggered my emotions in that situation, and how could I have changed my response?

Prayer Time

Dear God, thank you for the way we are remarkably made, including our emotions. Help me understand how my emotions can serve as communication tools not only to myself but also to those around me. Give me strength to manage my emotions. Amen.

Communication System

He rescues you from hidden traps,
shields you from deadly hazards.
His huge outstretched arms protect you—
under them you're perfectly safe;
his arms fend off all harm.

PSALM 91:1–4 MSG

I truly look forward to seeing many of my patients in the office. When I see Ben's name on my schedule for the day, I smile. Ben grapples with depression and anxiety as a result of his heart disease, which will require a transplant at some point, or the disease will take his life. He's lived with his sister and mother for some time now because his depression, anxiety, and heart disease have kept him from holding down a job and earning his own paycheck. It's a chaotic household because his sister and mother also struggle with their own mental health issues. Thankfully, Ben is a Jesus follower and, like many of my clients who are Jesus followers, once asked me this question: Is it a sin to be anxious?

Since I am not only an expert on the biological basis of anxiety and the stress response but also a Jesus follower, my answer to this common question is nuanced. The bottom line is no, I do not believe that anxiety is a sin; it is an emotion or feeling. Is joy a sin? Is grief a sin? Is surprise a sin? You've probably never even questioned whether these emotions are sinful because emotions and feelings are not inherently bad. Emotions are part of God's design for us, and they're tools that help us communicate to ourselves and others how we feel about an idea, an event, or a person. Then based on those feelings, an action or response is provoked. Emotions, like anxiety, are meant to prompt us to act. Anxiety is, therefore, a communicator.

The problem with anxiety as a communicator is that anxiety sometimes hears, receives, or interprets the message incorrectly. And if we act impulsively on our emotions or leave them unchecked, they have the potential to lead us to make sinful decisions. Therein lies the nuance of my initial answer. While it is difficult to learn how to navigate the space between feeling an emotion and acting on an emotion, it's our job as humans to closely examine our feelings and fact-check them for truth. As Jesus followers, it's our job to go one step further and cross-reference our emotions with God's truth.

Anxiety may warn us that we are in danger, but God assures us that we are safe. Anxiety may claim that we are unloved, but God promises that we are his treasure. Anxiety may paint our future bleak and hopeless, but God says, "I am your hope." He will dismantle every lie in his quest for our soul.

Anxiety, like all emotions, is a communicator that is, at times, unreliable. It's up to us to fact-check our anxiety.

Journaling Prompt

Recall a time when anxiety communicated a message of fear to me. Did I fact-check this fear, or did I act on this fear? What was the outcome? Next time my anxiety comes calling, how can I react differently?

Prayer Time

Dear God, thank you for building and composing within me an internal communication system of emotions. Help me recognize when my emotions are lying to me. Help me call out to you for wisdom and clarification instead of believing and acting on the lies of anxiety. I know that your way is best. Amen.

Unchanging Love

> *There is no power above us or beneath us—no power*
> *that could ever be found in the universe that can*
> *distance us from God's passionate love, which is lavished*
> *upon us through our Lord Jesus, the Anointed One!*
>
> ROMANS 8:39 TPT

My twelve-year-old daughter, Brooklyn Grace, is the perfect combination of me (intelligent, organized, ambitious) and my husband (creative, athletic, outdoorsy). She is forever covered in paint drippings from her bedroom art studio, and she bakes far more scrumptious treats for our family than I do.

My daughter, with her sweet, sweet soul, feels all of her feelings to the max, and those feelings are on display for everyone to see. It's part of what I love about her. You never have to question what she's feeling because it's written all over her face. When she's sad, tears stream down her cheeks, and sobs wrack her shoulders. When she's cheerful or amused, she lets out the most beautiful belly laugh I've ever heard, not to mention her smile alone is worth a million bucks. And when she's mad, she displays her anger pretty clearly too.

When Brooklyn feels intense or uncomfortable emotions, she sometimes struggles to understand that her feelings are not permanent. She thinks she'll always feel this way or that way, but this isn't true. I purposely remind her of that by saying, "It won't always be like this." The intensity of her emotions may be the reason that, somewhere along the way, Brooklyn got the impression that some emotions are good, and some emotions are bad. Or in other words, some emotions are more acceptable and pleasing to God and to those around us than other emotions.

Part of what I'm trying to teach her (and part of what I'm trying to learn myself) is that emotions are a normal part of our human existence. God created us this way on purpose, and no emotion is inherently good or bad. There are uncomfortable emotions, certainly, but emotions are not in and of themselves wrong, bad, or sinful. And if we label emotions as *bad*, we only intensify our feelings of guilt when we inevitably experience those "bad" emotions.

It's okay to be overwhelmed, angry, or despondent. We are humans with human emotions, and we are all doing the best we can. It's okay to have big feelings, and it's good to bring those feelings to God. He can handle our feelings of anger, sadness, and anxiety. He does not judge us or sort us into categories of good or bad based on our emotions. However turbulent our emotions may be, they do not cause him to love us any less; his love for us is unchanging.

What if God designed our emotional response system to direct us toward him? Joy can urge us closer to him. Grief can draw us closer to him. Fear can certainly drive us toward him, and sadness can encourage us to seek him out continually. He's beckoning and pleading with us to recognize our emotions for what they should be: a methodology for communication and a conduit for drawing near to him. The truth about who he is, his greatness, and how richly he loves us remains unchanged by our shifting emotions about him, the world, and our lives.

Sometimes we feel an emotion so strongly that we believe it will always feel this way, but the emotion will pass.

Journaling Prompt

Does the intensity of my emotions lead me to believe these feelings are permanent? What have I been taught about "good" emotions versus "bad" emotions? Where did I learn this? How can I unlearn what I have been taught about good emotions and bad emotions?

Prayer Time

Dear God, thank you for creating me with emotions, even though they run amok at times. Every second of every hour of every day, I need you. Help me understand that my emotions are part of the thoughtful, intentional, and intricate mind-body-spirit system that you created in me. Amen.

Control

*He knows us far better than we know ourselves...
and keeps us present before God. That's why we
can be so sure that every detail in our lives of love
for God is worked into something good.*

ROMANS 8:26–28 MSG

Like millions of parents, the responsibility of educating my tenth grader fell to me thanks to the single most anxiety-provoking event of 2020. You guessed it! The COVID-19 pandemic. I suddenly became a homeschool mom with all the responsibilities that come with that role, including creating lesson plans. The whole situation was complex, but the bottom line was that my son was at risk of failing three different classes in one term, which made my Type A, people-pleasing, Enneagram One heart shudder.

Not only did I lack control over the pandemic, but I also lacked control over the school's grading policies and my son's lack of intrinsic motivation. Not to mention I knew very little about the Spanish-American War and the conjugation of German verbs. This sudden, profound loss of control caused my anxiety to flare up.

Anxiety is a common response to uncertainty and a sense of loss of control. And the more out of control I feel over my circumstances, the more anxious I become. It's taking longer than I would like for me to learn this, but the reality is that no amount of control on my part can guarantee me peace of mind. Any guarantee of peace comes only from the Prince of Peace.

What *is* within my control? My thoughts, my behaviors, and my actions. What is outside my control? Everything else. I cannot control the circumstances I find myself in, but I can control how hard and fast I chase after Christ. I cannot control anything or anyone other than myself, but even understanding that reality does not stop me from trying to control whatever I can. But oh, how I try. Regardless, why do I think I can see and anticipate events better than God can? I'm not sure when, but at some point in my life, I began to believe that if I could manipulate or manage the details of a situation, I could also stave off the potential of a poor outcome.

The anxiety we feel is often a product of the fallen, broken world that we live in, which translates to a sense of a lack of control over our circumstances. However, loss of control is the flip side of freedom. I've learned to understand my anxiety as a side effect of the freedom and free will that I have in Christ. Consider this, friend: If we did not have freedom or free will to choose Christ, meaning our every move was predetermined, worry would cease to exist, right? It seems that the only guaranteed way to completely eradicate anxiety from our lives for good would be for our Creator to eliminate our ability to make decisions, leaving us without any say in our lives. Although it may come with the price of anxiety, I enjoy my gift of free will!

Let's learn to reject our instinct to control all of life's outcomes and instead place our complete trust in God. He is the truth that never changes and the One in true control. He watches over us with love and care, and he wants the best for us.

I will never be able to control all of my circumstances, but I can choose to continually chase after Christ. This much I *do* have control over.

Journaling Prompt

What is one area of my life that I'm attempting to control? Have I been able to obtain the desired results by maintaining control? How might my anxiety change if I were to give up some of that control?

Prayer Time

Dear God, help us to know that even when we cannot make sense of things, the reality is that you are weaving a story that we cannot yet see. Help us hand control over to you, for wherever you are there is freedom. Amen.

The Human Stress Response

Do not yield to fear, for I am always near.
Never turn your gaze from me,
for I am your faithful God.
I will infuse you with my strength
and help you in every situation.

ISAIAH 41:10 TPT

Sometimes when I look at my calendar, I feel overwhelmed. From soccer practice and school projects for the kiddos, to the launch of a major initiative at work, to a smattering of doctor appointments—my life is packed. All of these things are important in their own way. None of them can really be cut out or ignored, and I'm left wondering how I'm going to fit it all in *and* accomplish everything with excellence. Then my heart starts to flutter, and I know what that means: my anxiety is cropping up.

I've been in this situation countless times. My anxiety lies to me, trying to convince me that I'll never get it all done, that I'm spread too thin, and that I'm failing at being superwoman. These thoughts are so very familiar, and I tangle with my anxious imagination every day. Even though I know that I'm not in any real, mortal danger, my body seems to think the world is ending. My heart pounds. My neck stiffens, and my hands start to shake. I know all of the things to do in order to cope with my anxiety, so why is it so stinking difficult to control sometimes? The answer lies in our stress response.

Our stress response is an innate, instinctual response designed to be a life-saving tool. It's part of our sympathetic nervous system, which is a set of automatic responses to situations in which we feel unsafe. You may have heard of this triad of stress responses: fight, flight, or freeze. These responses are a systematic cascade of reactions instilled in us by our Creator. It's a brilliant design really. Our stress response kicks in, our adrenaline begins pumping, our heart rate climbs, and all of our internal systems work together with one singular goal: survival. Our sympathetic nervous system is fantastically skillful at keeping us alive in life-threatening situations. The catch, however, is that our stress response has a hard time distinguishing an acute, physical, life-threatening stressor from a non-life-threatening stressor.

We don't have to fight for our lives on a daily basis in the same way that humans who lived in the caveman days did. What we *do* have to deal with are non-life-threatening stressors, such as finances, relationships, and the uncertainties of the future. Nevertheless, our modern worries trigger the exact same release of stress hormones that life-threatening stressors trigger. That's why it's so difficult to control the stress response that is innate to our very makeup. Our bodies and emotions tell us that we are in just as much danger sifting through a stack of overdue bills while having an already overdrawn bank account as we would be when running away from a saber-tooth tiger.

What can we do when our bodies are trying to commandeer our minds? The best place to start is with prayer. Friend, he's available all of the time. He's our personal crisis hotline. Some people find comfort in using ice packs on their neck or face, practicing breath work, or performing muscle relaxation techniques to combat their body's uncomfortable stress response. With time and practice, we can learn to interpret what our bodies are trying to communicate to us without letting anxiety run the show.

We must learn to recognize when to trust our body's stress reaction. Just like our anxious thoughts can lie to us, our bodies can lie to us too. Next time you are feeling anxious (and trust me, there will be a next time), listen to what your body is trying to communicate to you, and then use both your wisdom and God's truth to plan your next move.

My innate stress reaction is outside of my control, but how I handle my anxiety is completely within my control.

Journaling Prompt

What are three physical symptoms of anxiety that I
experience? In the past, how have I dealt with these?
In the future, what new technique can I try instead?

Prayer Time

*Father God, thank you for creating a life-saving
system like my stress response. Help me learn to
recognize my emotions and physical symptoms and
distinguish between when I am truly in danger and
when I am not. Amen.*

DAY 6

Self-Talk

*You are the ones chosen by God, chosen for the high
calling of priestly work, chosen to be a holy people, God's
instruments to do his work and speak out for him, to tell
others of the night-and-day difference he made for you—
from nothing to something, from rejected to accepted.*

1 PETER 2:9–10 MSG

One of my favorite patients, whom we'll call Lacey, has Obsessive
Compulsive Disorder (OCD). OCD is an anxiety disorder in which
a person's anxious and intrusive thoughts rule his or her mind.
With OCD, a person becomes fixated on a particular fear or concern, and it's incredibly difficult to stop their spiraling thoughts.
Sometimes, the person engages in an action or behavior to lessen
the intensity of their thoughts. This battlefield of the mind can be
overwhelming to navigate. Lacey's particular case of OCD includes
a lot of self-deprecating thoughts. She second-guesses herself
constantly, and she beats herself up mentally with self-doubt and
negative self-talk, which is our topic for today.

The way we speak to ourselves inside our own heads and
the running dialogue taking place between our ears is called
"self-talk," and it can be positive or negative. The way we talk to
ourselves is usually derived from what we think and believe about
ourselves, which is a reflection of our self-regard, and it directly ties
to how we live out our lives. Every choice we make is a result of

whether we believe ourselves to be capable or incapable, adequate or inadequate, and worthy or worthless at our core.

Where do we get these beliefs about ourselves? Any number of places. Caregivers, parents, grandparents, spouses, teachers, employers, coworkers, and Instagram comments. Some of us grew up with exterior voices speaking negative, harmful things into our lives. Maybe someone said something to you when you were quite young, and their comment has stuck with you throughout your entire life. The input we receive in childhood, which may contribute to our anxiety as adults, is difficult to shake but not impossible.

We can't always control the sources of our input, but we can challenge the thoughts inside our heads. We can ask ourselves if we hold an opinion because we arrived at it on our own or if we are simply repeating what someone told us. It's our responsibility to take charge and set appropriate boundaries in all areas of our life—with our senses, our hearts, our minds, and our souls. Proverbs 4:23 charges us: "Pay attention to the welfare of your innermost being, for from there flows the wellspring of life" (TPT). We cannot allow the lies of our anxiety to speak louder than our identity in Christ. I often coach my patients on this: You are not your diagnosis. Your diagnosis is not your identity. There is a monumental difference between I *feel* anxious, and I *am* anxious.

Think about this question: Who holds the microphone inside your head? Is it a boss, a parent, a spouse, a former abuser, or your inner critic? Friend, if it's anyone other than God, you are listening to the wrong person. Scripture encourages us to keep our minds and thoughts fixed on him, anxious thoughts included. We are meant to take our warped philosophies about ourselves and our negative self-talk and shape them to who God says we are. Our verse today from 1 Peter 2 tells us that we are chosen, hand-selected, and beloved by our Savior. Not only that, but he also tasks us to speak on his behalf and be a living testimony to our healing.

The importance of positive self-talk cannot be overstated. Starting today, talk to yourself with more kindness. Believe in yourself a little more. Don't move about the world looking for evidence to support negative opinions of yourself. Pass the microphone to God! He has so much more in store for us if we choose to disregard our anxious thoughts, reverse our negative self-talk patterns, and look to him.

To help silence my anxious thoughts, I need to fire my inner critic and focus solely on truths from God.

Journaling Prompt

What are two lies that I believe about myself? What is/are the source(s) of these lies? How have these lies contributed to my anxious way of thinking?

Prayer Time

Dear God, thank you for always being present in my heart and soul, even when I don't feel you. Help me consistently include you in my thoughts, push aside anxious and negative self-talk, and learn the best way of thinking: the way you think about me. Amen.

Gratitude

> *When Daniel learned that the decree had been signed and posted, he continued to pray just as he had always done. His house had windows in the upstairs that opened toward Jerusalem. Three times a day he knelt there in prayer, thanking and praising his God.*
>
> DANIEL 6:10 MSG

I have a long commute to my office. On a good day, it takes about thirty-five minutes, but on a bad day, it takes seventy-five. When traffic is bad and I know I'm going to be late to work, it is one of the most dreadful feelings. My chest tightens. I *hate* being late to work. There's no back door for me to sneak through unnoticed; I have to walk directly through the lobby past the very patients (who managed to make it on time) who are waiting to see me. I imagine what my coworkers and my patients think of me. They are probably wondering how I can possibly give them advice about their lives when I can't even get my own life under control.

With that, my anxiety kicks off—my social anxiety in particular, the kind of anxiety where I become distinctly aware of the possibility that other people are watching me and that I might say or do something that would make them think less of me. My anxiety tells me that if I walk in late to the morning staff meeting, the heads of everyone who made it there on time will turn and stare me down, fueling my ever-present imposter syndrome. My anxiety tells me that if I start my day late, then I'll leave the office late, which means

I'll be late to pick up my daughter from the bus stop, which kicks off the never-ending self-deprecating dialogue in my head about how I'll never manage to be a great mom *and* enjoy a career. See how my anxiety can run amok? All of these negative thoughts from a bit of morning traffic.

Certainly, my tardiness to work is not the crisis we read about in today's verse from the book of Daniel, where he's received news that his life is at risk. Daniel lived in a time when a new law was passed that directly prohibited his religion, and if he continued to practice his spiritual beliefs, then he risked civil punishment. How did Daniel behave in his moment of personal crisis? He paused and prayed words of gratitude and praise. Daniel set a great example for us: When we are overwhelmed with anxiety, we, too, can pause and pray words of gratitude. In fact, regular practice of gratitude produces physiological changes to the structure of our brains.[3] Gratitude literally rewires our brains for the better.

Compared to Daniel's situation, my traffic example is trite. It's simply an everyday stressor that is entirely beyond my control, but it's a stressor that I can minimize with gratitude. When I find myself in these types of situations where my anxious thoughts start to get away from me, one of my most effective skills is to list off things for which I'm grateful. I talk back to my anxious thoughts, out loud, with statements of gratitude. In traffic, I say things like the following:

- Thank you, Lord, that I had enough gas in my car today to get me to work.

- Thank you, Lord, that my car started today.

- Thank you, Lord, that I'm going to a job that I truly enjoy.

- Thank you, Lord, for the education that enables me to work where I do.

- Thank you, Lord, that I live in a country where women are encouraged to seek out higher education.

- Thank you, Lord, that at the end of a hectic workday, I get to go home to a family I love.

And on and on it goes. This practice of gratitude distracts me from my anxious imagination and redirects my thoughts toward God. Before you know it, my anxious thoughts have lost their power over me. They may not be gone entirely, but they are not nearly as distressing.

We must rob anxiety of its power and control over us by interrupting anxiety with gratitude. Anxiety cannot survive in a land where gratitude rules. If Daniel, who faced the threat of death, can have the wherewithal to intentionally focus on gratitude, I can certainly do the same when stuck in traffic. Let's learn how to reroute, reframe, and refocus our anxious thoughts by contradicting them with gratitude.

A consistent practice of gratitude will soothe my anxiety and rewire me for the better.

Journaling Prompt

What is one of my most common everyday stressors?
How can I reverse the anxiety caused by that stressor
with a practice of gratitude? What am I grateful for
today? How can I place visual reminders throughout
my day to help me remember to be grateful?

Prayer Time

*Thank you, God, for your protection and the
good things you give me. Hold onto me; please
don't let me lose my way in all of this. It gets
really overwhelming sometimes. Help me to see
something good in everything because you have
made everything good. Amen.*

Blessed and Stressed

He got up and rebuked the wind and the raging waters;
the storm subsided, and all was calm. "Where is your
faith?" he asked his disciples. In fear and amazement
they asked one another, "Who is this? He commands
even the winds and the water, and they obey him."

LUKE 8:24–25 NIV

I stood in line at Hobby Lobby one day with my arms full of yarn on clearance. I've always had grand ideas of becoming the Pioneer Woman of handmade sweaters. So far, it hasn't worked out. Anyway, the spunky, lighthearted cashier seemed totally oblivious to the growing line that was forming, the impatience of customers, and the too-warm-for-comfort temperature in the store. When it was finally my turn to pay, I asked her how she was doing that day, to which she energetically quipped, "I'm just too blessed to be stressed, you know?" I smiled and nodded in agreement, gathering my bags, and she moved on to serve the next customer. As I walked to the parking lot, I kept thinking about that phrase: "too blessed to be stressed." The more I thought about it, the more I realized I didn't like it.

While I acknowledge the heart behind this catch phrase—focus on the positive, don't worry, express gratitude always—the insinuation is that you have to choose between feeling blessed and feeling stressed, as if you are only allowed to be one or the other but not both and certainly not at the same time. The insinuation is that you have to choose, and I disagree. You do not have to choose between two emotions that may seem contradictory. It's possible to experience both at the same time and in a valid way.

Let's use the example of becoming a parent. If you are a parent, perhaps you can recall the conflicting emotions you felt when you first walked out of that hospital, entrusted with a brand-new life. Chances are that you were flying high with joy but also weighed down by pounding fears of responsibility, uncertainty, and the future. Does the joy you felt mean that your fear was not warranted? Of course not. You felt both emotions equally and simultaneously. And both emotions were appropriate to your situation.

Picture this. You're looking forward to a relaxing Saturday afternoon at the lake with friends. A friend of a friend asks, "Can I invite my buddy to come along with us? He's getting his doctorate in theology, and he's full of the most interesting ideas." Let's say this sounds fun to you because you like the idea of learning from someone who has the potential to be an amazing conversationalist and teacher with the lake as a beautiful backdrop. (For me, this would be like going on a pontoon trip with Brené Brown!) Your plans go awry, though, when a storm appears out of nowhere while you're in the middle of the lake. You're not the strongest swimmer, so you become fearful within an instant. Then your teacher, with just a few words and a wave of the hand, supernaturally disbands the rain, wind, and thunder and calms the water. Your heart still pounds from moments ago when your life was in danger, but the threat is gone.

This is the situation the disciples found themselves in as we read our verses today from Luke 8:24–25. A friendly jaunt on the lake turns life-threatening, and then the danger quickly dissipates. It seems that the disciples were simultaneously afraid and amazed. Afraid of their circumstances (a wild, scary storm) yet in awe of the scene (our Savior calming the chaos). I can imagine how the disciples must have felt. How would you have felt? So full of wonder and so full of fright? Two seemingly contradicting emotions, jockeying around your heart to see which will be the strongest. I can imagine feeling that way because I feel that way most days.

It's possible to feel both gratitude and anxiety at the same time. We do not have to choose between one or the other. It's not an either-or situation; it's a both-and situation. It's possible to feel two seemingly conflicting emotions. More than that, it's *okay* to feel opposing emotions at the same time. God sees us and knows us because he made us. He made us as complex human beings with a vast network of emotions. He created us with the ability to feel multiple emotions at the same time. He does not expect us to choose between them. His goal for us is to experience all of our emotions, listen to them closely, and then manage those emotions in a healthy way.

I can feel blessed *and* stressed because my emotions do not override my faith in Christ.

Journaling Prompt

What two (or more) emotions am I feeling that may
seem to conflict with each other? Does this conflict
create in me a sense of guilt? How can I address this
going forward? How can I begin to recognize that all
of my emotions are valid?

Prayer Time

*Father God, thank you for wiring us as humans
who experience a range of emotions and often
experience that range of emotions at the same
time. Help us to examine those emotions, exert
control over those emotions, and allow any wayward
emotions to bring us closer to you. Amen.*

Input

*Keep your thoughts continually fixed on all that is
authentic and real, honorable and admirable, beautiful
and respectful, pure and holy, merciful and kind. And
fasten your thoughts on every glorious work of God,
praising him always.*

PHILIPPIANS 4:8 TPT

My mom was quite particular about the movies I watched
and the books I read when I was growing up. She restricted me
from consuming any content that was less than respectable. At
the time, her strictness frustrated me. My friends would talk about
their favorite parts of a television show, and I'd feel like an outcast
because it was a show that I was not allowed to watch. I tried to
negotiate, but my mom held fast. She would say, "Garbage in,
garbage out."

My mom understood that what I put in front of my eyeballs has
a direct influence on what goes on inside my head. She understood
that my input—whether it be in the form of media, photography,
movies, or the unsavory behavior or language of a peer—would
influence my thoughts, my interpretation of the world, and my
confidence. This concept applied to me certainly as a child, but it
applies to me even more powerfully now as an adult who tackles
anxiety daily. When anxious thoughts creep in, I remind myself to
check my input. If I feel anxious, there's a good chance that I've
gotten lazy or careless about what I'm allowing myself to read,

view, or listen to. That's why I choose to be cautious with what I allow to fill my senses. Garbage in, garbage out.

We read a long list of adjectives in our verse from Philippians today: authentic, real, honorable, admirable, beautiful, respectful, pure, holy, merciful, and kind. These same words should describe everything that we fill our senses with. If I'm filling my mind with anything that does not fall under these labels, it needs to go. To accomplish this, I ask myself, *What am I filling my eyes and my ears with? Am I filling my senses with positive influences, and healthful- ness? Am I filling my head with the Word and the promises of God, or am I spending too much time doom-scrolling on social media, soaking in the negativity of the news cycle?*

Friends, social media can be such dangerous territory. I don't want to paint social media as the bad guy. You might have learned about this book and me through social media. Theoretically, social media can be used for good, but more often than not, people use social media to brag, vent their negativity, or (this one hits home for me) as a trap for comparison. And we know that comparison is the thief of joy, right? If you think about it, social media is like fire. Used responsibly, it can cook you a warm meal; used recklessly, it can burn your house down.

What do you feel after time spent in the Word of God or in the company of a thoughtful friend? Peace? Love? Acceptance? Security? I sometimes experience questioning after reading Scripture, but I never feel dejected, beat down, insecure, or inad- equate like I do after an hour on social media. Those Instagram posts of a mother pictured alongside her four daughters, com- plete with matching fishtail braids and floral print dresses, inside their seemingly perfect, clean, well-designed home? Those posts make me feel more anxious and inadequate. The negative news cycle that's constantly predicting the demise of our country and its values? Those stories make me more anxious by encouraging catastrophizing. These types of input leave us feeling scared, fearful, criticized, insecure, less-than, and broken.

If I allow negative vibes into my environment, my thoughts are bound to become negative and exacerbate my anxiety. If I cultivate a peaceful environment in which I consciously protect my senses—sound, sight, and touch, then I'm less likely to become anxious. I can even use grounding techniques to further engage my senses. Grounding helps me hone in on my input. Here's a quick grounding exercise that I use frequently called the 5-4-3-2-1 technique. First, close your eyes and take three deep breaths. Then ask yourself in this moment:

- What are 5 things I can see?

- What are 4 things I can feel?

- What are 3 things I can hear?

- What are 2 things I can smell?

- What is 1 thing I can taste?

We don't always have control over our surroundings, and negativity sometimes wiggles its way into our lives despite our best efforts. That doesn't mean we can't strive for positivity. Paul tells us in Philippians how vital it is to focus on the good for the purpose of crowding out the bad. Remember to focus on what's positive, good, and true. Be intentional about filling your senses with things that build you up, not tear you down. Stop feeding the anxiety by cutting it off at the source, whatever that source may be. The world feeds us lies, but Scripture gifts us with truth.

I get to be in charge of my thoughts, and my thoughts come from my input. Control of my input will lead to control of my anxiety.

Journaling Prompt

Some days it feels as though my emotions are in charge, and I am simply along for the ride. What steps can I take to rewrite this narrative and intentionally fill my senses with goodness?

Prayer Time

Dear God, thank you for creating me with rich sensory abilities. Fill my senses with your goodness so that my heart remains at peace in the midst of my anxieties. Amen.

Patience

Lord, why do you seem so far away when evil is near?
Why have you hidden yourself when I need you the
most?... Yahweh, you have heard the desires of the
humble and seen their hopes. You will hear their cries
and encourage their hearts.

Psalm 10:1, 17 TPT

From a young age, I recall feeling anxious. I didn't have a name for it yet, but I remember feeling uneasy, uncomfortable, overwhelmed, and fearful. The feelings were foreign to me. In the evenings, my stomach would hurt, usually after dinner. My head hurt during school, and I bit my nails. These days, I no longer bite my nails, but I do chew on the insides of my cheeks, and my dentist has a lot to say about it. My anxiety became more intense as I grew older, but I started to learn how to put words to my experience.

I'm thirty-seven years old and still anxious. Sometimes I beat up on myself. I think, *Come on, Amanda, you should be over this by now. You're supposed to be an example to others on how to crush this.* Sometimes I beat up on God, asking him why he hasn't rescued me yet and what's taking him so long. How long have you been struggling with anxiety, friend? How long have you been praying for healing? How many times have you pleaded with God for relief or grown angry with him for not healing you yet? Have you felt overlooked, ignored, or forgotten? I have too. Like David the Psalmist in our reading for today, perhaps you wonder why God sometimes seems to hide himself during times of trouble. I don't have a definite answer as to why some of us wait years for healing from anxiety, or why some of us never find the healing we hope for during our time on earth, but I have a few ideas.

I have to wonder if God makes us wait because of the valuable lessons we learn during the struggle. Maybe God makes us wait because we'll have a smashing success story in the end, like the woman in Luke 8 who we will talk about another day. Rather than ask him why we battle anxiety, it's more productive to ask what God is trying to teach us. Ask yourself how God might use this situation to develop you, your character, and your resilience. Much of Scripture is devoted to the idea that God is deeply interested in refining our characters. James 1:2–4 is a perfect example: "Consider it pure joy, my brothers and sisters, whenever you face trials of many kinds, because you know that the testing of your faith produces perseverance. Let perseverance finish its work so that you may be mature and complete, not lacking anything" (NIV).

Does happiness come before strength? I don't believe so. I think it's the other way around. Happiness comes second; it's a consequence and reward for developing tenacity. When we are under pressure, we can grow in the depth of our understanding of God's character. Fear does to our faith what weights do to our muscles: it makes us stronger. I'm reminded of this fact every time I read this verse in 2 Corinthians:

> Though we experience every kind of pressure, we're not crushed. At times we don't know what to do, but quitting is not an option. We are persecuted by others, but God has not forsaken us. We may be knocked down, but not out. We continually share in the death of Jesus in our own bodies so that the resurrection life of Jesus will be revealed through our humanity. We consider living to mean that we are constantly being handed over to death for Jesus'

sake so that the life of Jesus will be revealed through our humanity. So, then, death is at work in us but it releases life in you. (2 Corinthians 4:8–12 TPT)

I am inclined to believe that God's way is best. He has more in store for us than we could ever dream up for ourselves. He's setting us up for a comeback even when we're heavy and weary with anxiety, and even when we feel like we've been waiting forever. What matters most is that we continue to move forward. Our direction is more important than our speed. Remain patient. Our every heartbeat says, "I'm a survivor."

Waiting time is not wasted time.

Journaling Prompt

Sometimes it feels as though my struggle with anxiety will last forever and that God doesn't hear me. What can I do to progress toward healing?

Prayer Time

Dear Father, thank you for the gift of waiting. Help me see that this is indeed a gift and that you have plans for me. Help my unbelief, help me press against my unbelief, and help me be consumed only with you. Amen.

CHECK-IN

#1

All I need to do is to call on you, Yahweh, the praiseworthy God. When I do, I'm safe and sound in you—delivered from my foes! For when the cords of death wrapped around me and torrents of destruction overwhelmed me, taking me to death's door, in my distress I cried out to you, the delivering God, and from your temple-throne you heard my troubled cry, and my sobs went right into your heart.

PSALM 18:3–6 TPT

*I*n your journal or notebook, record your responses to the following questions for reflection:

- Over the past ten days, what three teachings have impacted me most?

- What is God telling me about how I cope with my anxiety?

- With that in mind, how can I improve how I cope with my anxiety?

- What actionable steps can I take to improve how I handle my anxiety?

Identity

*He called you out of darkness to experience his
marvelous light, and now he claims you as his very own.
He did this so that you would broadcast his glorious
wonders throughout the world.*

1 PETER 2:9 TPT

Anxiety lies to me every day. It sometimes lies about my circumstances and how my future, near or far, will turn out. The lies are most often about myself—that I'm not good enough, not doing enough, or lacking in some way. Or that if I don't lock my car doors the second I get in, I'll get carjacked; that since my child took five dollars from my purse without asking, they are destined for a life of crime; that my introverted nature is less valuable to society compared to a person who is gregarious; that being tall makes me less feminine; that my husband will become bored of me since my hair is thinning, my middle is thickening, and my eyelids are wrinkling.

The rhetoric of the world and the tangle of my anxious mind are so loud sometimes that they drown out the ever-patient reminders of God. How much of our anxiety is rooted in misunderstanding or forgetting our identity? It turns out that, for me at least, a great deal of my anxiety comes from identity confusion. I get it so, so wrong when I listen to anxiety's opinion of who I am that I forget my true identity: a beloved child of God. We know from Scripture that God has called and created us, and I refuse to believe that he's a Creator of junk. Our verse for today from 1 Peter tells us we are chosen by

God for a higher calling; we have the potential of going from nothing to something. From rejected to accepted.

Anxiety is a liar, especially when it comes to our understanding of who we are. Anxiety says we have to perform. Jesus tells us to simply love God and others. Anxiety tells us we're not good enough. Jesus tells us we're not enough without him, but he freely gives himself to us with complete love and grace. The anxiety of many people (myself included) derives from a perception that we're failing or not measuring up to some perfectionist ideal that doesn't even exist in real life. That is fake news. We must remember who God tells us we are: beloved, treasured, and valued. He knows his way around our hearts, and we can trust him to tell the truth.

What does God have to say about who you are? Here's a brief list:

- Created in his very likeness (Genesis 1:27)

- His daughter (Galatians 3:26)

- Holy and blameless (Ephesians 1:4)

- Chosen (Ephesians 1:11)

- Redeemed and forgiven (Ephesians 1:7)

- A citizen of heaven (Philippians 3:20)

- A new creation in him (2 Corinthians 5:17)

- Fearfully and wonderfully made (Psalm 139:14)

- Secure under his protection (John 10:28)

- Accepted (Romans 15:7)

- Valuable (Matthew 6:26)

- Free from his condemnation (Romans 8:1)

- A dwelling for his spirit (1 Corinthians 6:19)

- Beloved (1 John 3:1)

When anxiety comes calling, clap back with the truth: you are the very treasure of God. You are who he says you are: chosen, beloved, restored, and reclaimed. If God, who sees us truly and knows all of our flaws, still chooses to extend his grace, how can we not extend it to ourselves? Friend, let's show ourselves the same compassion that God shows us. Let's remind ourselves daily of our identity in him. Over time, this practice will hush the roar of anxiety's lies.

Anxiety is a liar: Christ is the truth.

Journaling Prompt

What are some of the lies that my anxiety leads me to believe about myself? What does the Bible have to say about who I am? How can I change my thinking so that I focus on the truth instead of the lies?

Prayer Time

Dear God, thank you for loving me and surrounding me every day with your truth. You are greater than all of my anxieties. Help me embrace this and never forget that in you I am enough. Amen.

Smart Decision-Making

I am ready to fall,
And my sorrow is continually before me.
For I admit my guilt;
I am full of anxiety because of my sin.

PSALM 38:17–18 NASB

I have been living at the intersection of faith and mental health for eight years. Once I learned to manage my anxiety, I wanted to do everything I could to help others on their journey to recovery. This, among other things, is what we as Jesus followers are called to do: when we survive something, we are obligated to come alongside others and help them. And it turns out that a lot of people in the church struggle with depression and anxiety. Jesus followers don't always feel the freedom to speak up about their mental health, so I was truly thrilled to become a voice for a population of people who wanted to address their anxiety through the lens of faith.

A funny thing happened. As I started speaking and teaching more about faith and mental health, I quickly noticed that people consistently asked me this question: Is anxiety a sin? It puzzled me. Somewhere along the way, Jesus followers have been taught that anxiety is a sin (*sin* meaning a deliberate evil act that goes against God's best for us and thus separates us from God). The idea that anxiety is a sin has led to a great deal of shame and blame for those of us who earnestly love and seek after God but who also sincerely struggle with anxiety. Because of this notion of anxiety as a sin, many Christians have been reluctant to seek help for fear of judgment, criticism, embarrassment, and blame.

The question of whether anxiety is a sin is a subject that I am quite passionate about. It fires me up. While this conversation has some nuances that we don't have space to explore in this devotional, my short answer to this question is no, I do not believe anxiety is a sin. I personally do not recall ever being taught about that one commandment, *Thou Shalt Not Be Anxious*, do you? What I do want you to understand though is that anxiety can result from sin, primarily from poor choices. Please hear my heart on this: I am not saying that anxiety is your fault. Anxiety is a biological process that has been with you since birth, and it was designed in you by God for a purpose (remember what we learned on day 3?). What I *am* saying is that we can often decrease our levels of anxiety or decrease the likelihood of experiencing it by making good decisions.

The beauty of free will has the potential to land us in heaps of trouble. However, smart decision-making—when it comes to how we spend money, how we behave, how we choose relationships, how we set boundaries, and how we use our time—can spare us from heartache and anxiety down the road. How can we make better decisions? By surrounding ourselves with people who make good decisions (Proverbs 13:20), by seeking input from other trusted sources (Proverbs 15:22), and through prayer (James 1:5).

> If you want to grow in wisdom,
> spend time with the wise.
> Walk with the wicked
> and you'll eventually become just like them.
> (Proverbs 13:20 TPT)

> Your plans will fall apart right in front of you
> if you fail to get good advice.

But if you first seek out multiple counselors,
you'll watch your plans succeed. (Proverbs 15:22 TPT)

And if anyone longs to be wise, ask God for wisdom and he will give it! He won't see your lack of wisdom as an opportunity to scold you over your failures but he will overwhelm your failures with his generous grace. (James 1:5 TPT)

We also have assurance that no matter what poor choices we have made, Christ will never, ever give up on us:

I live with the confidence that there is nothing in the universe with the power to separate us from God's love. I'm convinced that his love will triumph over death, life's troubles, fallen angels, or dark rulers in the heavens. There is nothing in our present or future circumstances that can weaken his love. There is no power above us or beneath us—no power that could ever be found in the universe that can distance us from God's passionate love, which is lavished upon us through our Lord Jesus, the Anointed One! (Romans 8:38–39 TPT)

We are fully known, with all our faults and flaws, and still he wants us. Nothing we have done, or will do, can separate us from him. He resurrects us every day. Another piece of good news? It's never too late to start making better decisions, friend.

Smart decision-making helps to minimize and prevent anxiety.

Journaling Prompt

What is one poor decision that I made in the past that I now regret and which causes me anxiety? How can I make better choices in the future? Who are the trusted people in my life whom I can call on to help me make better decisions?

Prayer Time

Father, thank you for holding me and loving me, even when I make mistakes or bad choices. Thank you for your grace upon grace. Help me to seek you first, always, when facing a tough situation. I need your guidance in making the right decisions so that my heart and mind will be at peace. I want to be with you. Amen.

Words of Encouragement

*Anxious fear brings depression,
but a life-giving word of encouragement
can do wonders to restore joy to the heart.*

PROVERBS 12:25 TPT

*N*othing thrills me more than witnessing life-change in my patients. I work with beautiful people who are changing, growing, and doing the hard work of recovery to experience health and wellness. The grit of the human spirit stuns me every day, and I'm both privileged and grateful to have a front-row seat to it all. I truly love my job, and I know that the work I perform in the mental health field is exactly what God created me to do.

My job can also be draining. I have difficult yet necessary conversations with people about their unhealthy patterns or choices and unreasonable expectations. Typically, on my long commute home, I replay and review every conversation, every interaction, and every email. I critique and second-guess myself, worrying whether I have offered poor oversight, or I rehearse how I could have worded a piece of advice in a more coherent way. I consider how unfair life is for some of my patients. The cumulative load of my day is often heavy, and I'll admit that on weekdays I'm not always in the best mood when I walk through the back door of our house.

Do you ever come home at the end of the workday in a similar state? Feeling heavy and weighed down? When this happens, I know I'm not the best version of myself. I'm definitely not the person I want to be for my family. More often than not, those emotions fade away when I see my husband, Joseph. He is, more than any other person in my life, an encouragement to me. A quick, soft kiss on the cheek, a smile that reaches to his eyes, and a simple "Hey babe, I missed you today" from him is sometimes all it takes for my anxious heart to begin to quiet, for my fear to start to dissipate, and for my insecurities to start to dissolve.

Words are powerful. I experience the joy and relief described in our verse today from Proverbs, as well as Psalm 94:19, on a daily basis as a result of my husband's encouragement: "Whenever my busy thoughts were out of control, the soothing comfort of your presence calmed me down and overwhelmed me with delight" (TPT). I recognize what a gift it is to have an encouraging husband, and I understand that not everyone looks forward to coming home to their family. For many people, their family is one of their biggest anxiety triggers. Perhaps someone else in your life can be a source of soothing comfort. Who can you turn to for consistent positive encouragement to help you quiet your anxious thoughts? The best part of all is that words of encouragement don't have to come from others. We can use kind, positive words on ourselves—anytime, anywhere. Remember that skill of positive self-talk?

Lastly, consider how you can be a voice of encouragement for someone else. There's no reason for us not to make an effort to share kind words with one another. We may never know every detail of a person's life or every thought inside of their head, but the kind words we can share with someone who is struggling cost us nothing and may even comfort them in a time of need.

A kind, encouraging word can bulldoze my anxious thoughts and flatten my anxieties.

Journaling Prompt

Who is my biggest encourager? What are the two most encouraging statements this person has said to me, and did those encouragements help soothe my anxiety? If yes, how? If no, why not? Who can I encourage today?

Prayer Time

Dear God, thank you for the gift of communication and rich language. How wise you are to invent life-giving community. Help us use our tongues to praise you and lift each other up during times of grief and anxiety. Amen.

Hope

*Against all odds, when it looked hopeless, Abraham
believed the promise and expected God to fulfill it…
And because he was mighty in faith and convinced that
God had all the power needed to fulfill his promises,
Abraham glorified God!*

ROMANS 4:18, 20–21 TPT

Almost every day, a beautiful soul who has struggled with
anxiety for years walks into my office feeling defeated, weary, and
worn. She's doing everything I've asked her to do, and yet she
continues to struggle. She'll say, "I'm losing hope," and my heart
sinks to the floor. I know firsthand how insurmountable the battle
against chronic anxiety can seem. It feels like drowning sometimes.
We read over and over in Psalms about the emotion that comes as
a result of waiting for healing:

> God, my God, come and save me!
> These floods of trouble have risen higher and higher.
> The water is up to my neck!
> I'm sinking into the mud with no place to stand,
> and I'm about to drown in this storm.
> I'm weary, exhausted with weeping.
> My throat is dry, my voice is gone,
> my eyes are swollen with sorrow,

and I'm waiting for you, God, to come through for me.
(Psalm 69:1–3 TPT)

God, my God! Why would you abandon me now? Why do
you remain distant, refusing to answer my tearful cries in the
day and my desperate cries for your help in the night? I can't
stop sobbing. Where are you, my God? (Psalm 22:1–2 TPT)

Come close to me and give me your answer.
Here I am, moaning and restless.
I'm preoccupied with the threats of my enemies
and crushed by the pressure of their opposition.
They surround me with trouble and terror.
In their fury they rise up against me in an angry uproar.
(Psalm 55:2–3 TPT)

David the Psalmist feels like he's drowning. He's in a storm, a
lovely, gracious tempest. He feels completely overwhelmed by his
circumstances, crowded in on every side. Despite all of the sadness and desperation we read in David's words, it seems to me like
he's holding on to a glimmer of hope. Hope is a funny thing. The
slightest hint of it can overrule the thickest of sorrow and grant us
the strength and courage to face another day. It can be elusive at
times, but it's also readily available if we want it. It may not always
be the logical thing to possess, as it can require so much faith, but
it often requires so little sacrifice. Hope has the power to drown
out doubt and embolden us to stay the course.

The New International Version of today's Scripture from
Romans 4 reads, "Against all hope, Abraham in hope believed"
(v. 18). Abraham had no logical reason to believe that he would
be the patriarch of generations given his wife's age. Nevertheless,
Abraham had hope when no hope was to be had. It blows my
mind. I see in Abraham a stubborn hope that upended his own
unbelief in the power of God's promise despite it defying all sense
of logic. Abraham deliberately and consciously chose hope. What

blows my mind even further is that Abraham didn't even have the written words of God to refer to like we do today. He couldn't whip out of a copy of the Scriptures and read about God's promises and character. It seems that Abraham's faith in the source of his hope was very great indeed.

You may feel as though it makes little to no sense for you to continue pursuing relief from anxiety. You may have been dealing with it for months, years, or decades, and you are probably weary, worn, and ready to give up. Please don't give up, friend. Giving up won't get you where you want to be, and fear only serves to magnify the enemy. It takes hard-nosed self-discipline to fix our eyes on what is unseen, to push forward when nothing makes sense, to hold on to hope, and to say, *I trust you, God*. You are capable of persistence.

When our anxiety feels overwhelming, our next steps look fuzzy, and our path appears unclear, we can cling to a wild hope in a lovely and beautiful Savior, who is hope himself.

Journaling Prompt

If I'm being honest with myself, have I given up hope
in my battle with anxiety? What or who am I relying
on to provide me hope? What steps can I take to
push forward in my battle with anxiety?

Prayer Time

Dear God, thank you for being my living hope,
who cares for every single detail of my life. Help me
to overcome the doubts my anxiety creates and help
me to believe that relief from anxiety is possible.
I know you can make me brave. Amen.

Patterns

> *We use our powerful God-tools for smashing warped philosophies, tearing down barriers erected against the truth of God, fitting every loose thought and emotion and impulse into the structure of life shaped by Christ.*
>
> 2 CORINTHIANS 10:5 MSG

As I walk from my car to my office every workday, I mentally work through serious symptoms of impostor syndrome. With each step I think to myself, *What am I doing here? I'm unqualified. I'm such a fraud.* This kicks off a stream of anxious thoughts, worsened by the fact I do not feel as though I can talk about this with colleagues (what if they confirm my self-doubts?). Imposter syndrome is discussed by the American Psychological Association as a feeling of inadequacy, self-doubt, questioning one's own qualifications and abilities, and a sense of *what gives me the right to be here?* Imposter syndrome and the anxiety it elicits has a lot to do with our self-talk habits and our identity in Christ.

We discussed the importance of self-talk on day 6, but its power cannot be underestimated. If we speak to ourselves kindly, we set ourselves up for grace. If we beat up on ourselves, we invite a spiral of anxious thoughts. Our self-talk habits and our beliefs about our identity are joined at the hip. As we move forward in recovery from anxiety, we learn that our opinion of ourselves is of utmost importance because we live out of that mindset. Proverbs conveys a hint of this concept: "As [a man] thinketh in his heart, so is he" (23:7 KJV).

My anxious, self-talk patterns used to sound like this: *You are not good enough. You'll never be good enough. You really messed that up. Why aren't you more disciplined? Why can't you be a better example? What if this doesn't work out? Who do you think you are?* Now my self-talk patterns are focused on overcoming my anxiety and sound like this: *I am nothing without him, and since I have him, I have everything. I am secure in who God tells me I am. He is in control, and he has my best interest in mind. I am his beloved, and he loves me so much that he sacrificed everything for me.* Even David, author of the oft-quoted Psalms below, has to wrestle with his internal dialogue and remind himself of whom he should be trusting and relying on:

> So then, my soul, why would you be depressed? Why would you sink into despair? Just keep hoping and waiting on God, your Savior. For no matter what, I will still sing with praise, for living before his face is my saving grace! (Psalm 42:5 TPT)

> I will say to my soul, "Don't be discouraged; don't be disturbed, for I fully expect my Savior-God to break through for me. Then I'll have plenty of reasons to praise him all over again." Yes, he is my saving grace! (Psalm 43:5 TPT)

> Bless the Lord, O my soul, and all that is within me, bless his holy name! Bless the Lord, O my soul, and forget not all his benefits. (Psalm 103:1–2 ESV)

Friend, if you feel ashamed of yourself, that doesn't mean that Jesus is ashamed of you too. Not a single day has passed in which God panicked and thought, *Darn. She's ruined everything I had planned for her.* David struggled with anxiety like most all of us do, and he understood where to turn in the midst of it all: our Christ. Our loving Savior waits with bated breath for the moment when we abandon our self-deprecating internal dialogue and instead turn our anxieties over to him.

As I move about the world, I must learn to harness my negative self-talk and reframe it within the context of God's love.

Journaling Prompt

What are two of the most commonly recurring
anxious thoughts or negative self-talk patterns
that I experience? How can I rephrase or reframe
these patterns?

Prayer Time

*Father God, thank you for loving me through my
anxiety. You love me more than I will ever fully
understand and probably more than I will ever love
myself. You are great and abundantly patient. Help
me to fill my head with positive self-talk that reflects
your definition of who I am and whose I am. Amen.*

Personal Needs

Don't let worry enter your life. Live above the anxious cares about your personal needs. People everywhere seem to worry about making a living, but your heavenly Father knows your every need and will take care of you.

LUKE 12:29–30 TPT

Jesus spoke directly on the subject of anxiety only a handful of times, and our reading for today is one of them. It comes from a passage in Luke chapter 12, and in it, Jesus uses the example of birds as an illustration of a soul that lives without worry for the future but instead trusts that everything will work out. Jesus encourages us to discard our anxieties, especially those related to our basic needs, because he will provide for us no matter what the circumstances may be.

This verse can be difficult to read for many who struggle with chronic anxiety because this verse has been weaponized—perhaps by well-intentioned loved ones but weaponized nonetheless—as an example of how people who worry are sinning. I may be alone in this, but this verse has honestly never even brought much comfort to me.

Of course, the flowers and the birds are quite lovely in their carefree state, Jesus. I do not doubt that I am more beloved to God than the animals and plants, but I doubt that those birds have the same worries that I do. The flowers of the field and the birds of the air do not have to consider how they will pay for the extra car insurance required for my sixteen-year-old. The flowers and the birds don't have to worry about my mom's cancer, my son's failing grades, or my constant fear that my husband will die before me, and I'll be left alone forever. Isn't it possible that the birds are care-free because they have so little to worry about? (I can't know for sure. I'm not a bird.) The comparison simply falls flat for me.

With these words recorded in the book of Luke, Christ is offering an invitation, an encouragement, not a command. Let's look closely and consider exactly what worries Jesus cautions us about in this verse: food, clothing, and finances. Why does he discourage us from worrying about these needs in particular? Because our lives are "infinitely more" than the food we eat or the clothing we wear (Luke 12:23 TPT). Food, clothing, and money, though necessary in certain amounts for life, are not what life is about.

Life is about loving God and loving others. As I seek his kingdom and serve others first, I will find that all of my needs are provided for—not in a transactional way but rather in a heart-changing, perspective-shifting way. My choice to focus on good grace and service to others quiets my anxieties. Each and every day he will supply my needs as I seek his kingdom passionately, above all else.

Christ makes himself available to us at any and every moment. Like a parent who comforts their child by saying, "Don't worry, we'll figure this out," Christ says to us, "Don't worry, I've got this." With every anxious thought that runs through our head, he hopes we will come to him so that he can assure us firsthand of his plan for our safety.

Life is about seeking God's kingdom first. Everything else will fall into place, including my peace of mind.

Journaling Prompt

What is one example from the past week when my anxiety got away from me? How long did it take for me to pray about my worry? How can I bring Jesus into my worry process earlier next time?

Prayer Time

Father God, help me to continue to trust you with all my worries, big and small. I know that you care about each and every one of my anxious thoughts. Nothing is too unimportant for your concern. You invite me to include you in my anxieties for the very purpose of building my trust in the outcomes you have planned for me. Help me to reach out to you first in every worry. Amen.

God's Plans

*Which one of you by worrying
could add anything to your life?*

MATTHEW 6:27 TPT

One of my first experiences with anxiety as an adult (at least that I can remember) was when I first learned I was pregnant with my son, Alexander. Most every first-time mom has a brush with anxiety; it's a normative human reaction, but learning of my pregnancy with Alex was more intense than what many might expect. I was only twenty years old, newly engaged (to my husband, Joseph), recently moved back in with my mom and pastor father, just beginning nursing school, and anything but ready to be pregnant.

Standing in the bathroom on the first floor of the research building on the University of Cincinnati's campus, where I was working at the time, I stared at the pregnancy test result: positive. I can still feel the tsunami of emotions: fear, worry, dread, unease, and loss of control. Catastrophic what-ifs started to flood my mind: *What if my dad gets fired from his pastoral role when his church leaders find out? What if Joseph leaves me because of this? What if I'm unable to finish school and can't support a baby?* What if, what if, what if. Of course, none of these things happened.

I know all of the cliché lines of comfort: God is in control; he loves me unendingly; he's near to the brokenhearted and crushed in spirit, and he has big, grand plans to prosper me. These are promises I've heard my entire life as a Jesus follower. But in particularly tough times, my anxiety is deafening. How has worrying ever served me? Has worrying ever paid off for me or added any value to my life, as Jesus asks in our Scripture reading for today? Has my worry truly changed an outcome or reversed something scary into something positive? I can't recall a single instance of any of this happening. What I *can* recall (and easily) is the amount of sleep I've lost from racing thoughts. I can recall all of the social gatherings to which I was invited but decided not to attend, only to sit at home obsessing about my decision. I can effortlessly rattle off all the moments that had potential for joy, but instead I allowed my anxiety to steal that joy from me.

Personally, one of my go-to coping skills for my anxiety is control. Whenever I am worried about an outcome, my knee-jerk reaction is to exert as much control over the situation as possible, but this plan fails, predictably, because the control never belonged to me in the first place. It belongs to Jesus. Jesus has already destroyed everything that has the power to take me out. Why do I struggle to accept this gift?

We do not have to fight on our own. Let's be done with lost sleep and shattered plans. We've spent too much time preparing ourselves for worst-case scenarios and attempting to manipulate our circumstances to avoid the disastrous endings we've orchestrated in our minds. When anxiety comes calling, tell her, "I refuse to miss out on the life that God has planned for me any longer."

Let's give up the glass-half-empty perspective that anxiety wants us to believe and consciously choose to focus on the good, the certain, and the true. Let's abandon the control that was never ours to begin with for the plan he has for us: his big-picture, master plan.

Even when my anxiety is at its loudest,
I am capable of amplifying God's voice.
I want to hear his voice above all others.

Journaling Prompt

What is an example of when I carried a worry for something that was out of my control, and the very outcome I dreaded never came to pass? Did my act of worrying or attempt to control change the outcome at all?

Prayer Time

Dear God, I know you are bigger than my biggest worry—and still, it's hard to drown out my anxious thoughts. Remind me of the plans you have for me, over and over again, because I'm forgetful, Lord. Help me to hand over control of my life to you, willingly and readily. Amen.

Persistence

*Ask, and the gift is yours. Seek, and you'll discover.
Knock, and the door will be opened for you. For every
persistent one will get what he asks for. Every persistent
seeker will discover what he longs for. And everyone
who knocks persistently will one day find an open door.*

MATTHEW 7:7–8 TPT

At the time of my writing these words, I've been married for seventeen years. We have a sixteen-year-old son and a twelve-year-old daughter. My husband and I married at the tender age of twenty, and if you do the math, then you'll see why I feel so ill-equipped to parent both a teen and a tween. At thirty-seven, I've only just now figured out a few of life's secrets for myself. How am I supposed to effectively parent a teen and successfully catapult him into the world?

Here's one thing I *do* know about parenting: kids need to hear the word no. The fad of free-range parenting is among the worst parenting philosophies a parent can choose. Giving a child everything they ask for may bring temporary peace but will result in character flaws down the road. A loving parent takes care of their children and gives them what is best, even if the best is telling them, "Not right now."

Many well-meaning Christian writers and bloggers, trying to encourage me in my fight against anxiety, refer to Jesus' wonderful words in our Scripture reading for today from Matthew. (Every day I wish the Bible included more of the words Jesus spoke to those around him, don't you?) Anyone fighting a seemingly uphill battle will turn to this verse. It is, after all, a promise of how much we as children are loved by our Father God.

As I persisted in my recovery from anxiety, these particular words from Matthew discouraged me. They made the solution seem so simple: if I wanted healing, then all I had to do was ask for it. Believe me, I did not hesitate to ask God for healing. I asked, begged, pleaded—I even supplicated (one of the most Christian-y things a person can do!). Relief did not come, and of course I struggled to understand why because according to Matthew 7:7, anything I want is mine; I simply have to ask.

Now I realize the error in my simplistic thinking and read this verse with a different perspective and through a clearer lens. When I read about the wonderful gifts that God has promised me, I no longer believe that gift is healing; I believe the gift is knowledge. Knowledge of deep truths, knowledge of him, knowledge of relationship, and knowledge of my purpose.

These words in Matthew are a stark reminder of how vital it is to hold on to hope in our battle with anxiety. Dogged persistence pays off, and eventually, healing will come, even if it's not within the time frame or in the form for which we'd hoped. We read in Luke 21:19, "Stand firm with patient endurance and you will find your souls' deliverance" (TPT).

Just like I have to tell my often impatient children, "No, not right now," God is saying, "No, not yet" to our begging for relief. He wants us to have the knowledge that can only come through the struggle. He wants us to develop patience and endurance because only then will we find true rescue. God teaches us through our struggles, and our struggles become a masterclass.

When it comes to my struggle with anxiety and uncertainty, I must remember that it won't always be like this.

Journaling Prompt

Over the past six months, what were two of my
most anxiety-provoking circumstances? In the
midst of those circumstances, did it feel like things
would never get any better? Was that true? Did my
circumstances change, or did my feelings about my
circumstances change?

Prayer Time

*Dear God, thank you for your promises through your
son, Jesus. Please help me to interpret your Word
correctly, to understand your master plan for me,
and above all else to understand my purpose while
I am waiting for healing. Help me not to give up on
you. Amen.*

Mindfulness

*Refuse to worry about tomorrow, but deal with each
challenge that comes your way, one day at a time.
Tomorrow will take care of itself.*

MATTHEW 6:34 TPT

Once upon a time, my husband and I were wedding photographers, which is a far cry from what we do now. Planning a wedding and getting married are named as some of the most stress-inducing events in a person's life.[4] We would book out a couple's wedding date months and sometimes even years in advance. Part of our success in the wedding biz, before we decided to retire and pursue other passions, was that we were good at planning. Planning by definition involves considering events and situations that will take place many days, weeks, months, or even years in the future in an effort to avoid undesirable outcomes.

I am a planner. And by *planner* I mean that I obsessively review the most minute details of every possible change in circumstance. Planning is one of the ways I learned to cope with my anxiety. I balance, add buffer, and plan out what I can so that when an unexpected stressor pops up, I feel organized and prepared to handle it.

The passage from Matthew that we read today gives us the words of Jesus telling us to refuse to worry about tomorrow. Initially, that seems like a fairly strong command, but let's look closer. Is this a literal command from Jesus to not think about tomorrow, to not plan ahead, and to only be responsible for today?

That does not sound like reasonable advice. It seems irresponsible for me not to plan what time to arrive at work tomorrow morning since I have patients waiting for me. As a wedding photographer, it seems irresponsible not to block out a date on my calendar next year when a bride is paying me a significant amount of money to show up with a camera.

Instead, this passage from Matthew is introducing us to the concept of mindfulness to help us avoid the habit of catastrophizing. *Mindfulness* can be an intimidating or off-putting word to Christians, especially given that mindfulness practices are often combined with breath work and meditation. Meditation can feel like an Eastern practice and conjures up images of a plump Buddha sitting cross-legged on the ground. I get it.

Here's how I understand mindfulness. It is the act of slowing down or practicing stillness for the purpose of focused attention, intention, and awareness. The practice of mindfulness helps us to slow the breakneck speed at which we move through life so that we can focus on the task directly in front of us. Meditation, which is often used interchangeably with mindfulness, helps us break away from the path of simply allowing senses and emotions to blindly rule our lives. All too often, I become overwhelmed in part because my senses were overloaded; mindfulness meditation helps me decompress.

Jesus is telling us here in Matthew to slow down, be present, don't get too wrapped up in what's to come tomorrow, tackle today's to-do list first, and take things day by day. The idea of being still and calm reminds me of a verse in Psalm 46: "Be still, and know that I am God; I will be exalted among the nations, I will be exalted in the earth" (v. 10 NIV).

A different translation of Psalm 46:10 phrases it this way: "Surrender your anxiety! Be silent and stop your striving and you will see that I am God. I am the God above all the nations, and I will be exalted throughout the whole earth" (TPT). Stillness comes before peace, stillness comes before worship, and stillness comes before knowledge: "Come back to me! By returning and resting in me you will be saved. In quietness and trust you will be made strong" (Isaiah 30:15 TPT). It seems that one of the best ways to become stronger, especially in our battle with anxiety, is to become quieter.

Practicing mindfulness and stillness can soothe my anxiety by shifting my awareness to him and crowding out the worries of tomorrow—even if only for a moment.

Journaling Prompt

What is one example in the past week when my anxiety caused me to feel frantic and overwhelmed? Was I feeling overwhelmed in part because I faced multiple stressors at once? Was I feeling overwhelmed in part because my senses were overloaded? In moments like those, how can I use the tools of mindfulness and stillness before God to calm my anxious thoughts?

Prayer Time

Dear God, thank you for the gift of time. Even though the amount of time we have on our hands can be a stressor, help us to recognize what a gift time can be when used wisely. Help us to wisely structure our days to be centered around you so that we may bring you glory with our calm minds and focused hearts. Amen.

The Purpose of Pain

We continue to shout our praise even when we're hemmed in with troubles, because we know how troubles can develop passionate patience in us, and how that patience in turn forges the tempered steel of virtue, keeping us alert for whatever God will do next.

ROMANS 5:3 MSG

The question of why someone has anxiety is one I answer almost every day. As a clinician, I have the answer for that, although it's multifaceted. As a Christian, the answer is even more complex. In the context of anxiety, there are a lot of answers to this question, and one of them is that it often takes heartache to change and grow. Developing strength through adversity is an age-old formula. Pain teaches us.

In short, the answer is this: God is more concerned with developing our character than providing a quick fix to our problems. He's not interested in removing our struggle or resolving our circumstances without some sort of growth on our part. If he were to wave a magic wand and erase all of our worries (which, let's face it, is an attractive option), chances are we would continue throughout adulthood with the patience and temperament of a toddler, never developing or reaching a state of wisdom and maturity. We would tantrum our way through the hard parts of life, stomping our feet to demand immediate resolution.

In our reading today from Romans, Paul tells us a better way. Practicing patience in waiting and shouting God's goodness in the midst of uneasiness may seem counterintuitive, but it will actually draw us closer to him and keep us more in tune with his will for us. Every day that we struggle with anxiety is another opportunity to learn. Every second spent with an anxious thought is one that could otherwise bring us closer to God in prayer.

We read in 2 Corinthians 4:17 about the long-term payout for our struggles while we live here on Earth: "We view our slight, short-lived troubles in the light of eternity. We see our difficulties as the substance that produces for us an eternal, weighty glory far beyond all comparison" (TPT). I especially love this particular translation of this verse:

> We're not giving up. How could we! Even though on the outside it often looks like things are falling apart on us, on the inside, where God is making new life, not a day goes by without his unfolding grace. These hard times are small potatoes compared to the coming good times, the lavish celebration prepared for us. There's far more here than meets the eye. The things we see now are here today, gone tomorrow. But the things we can't see now will last forever. (2 Corinthians 4:16–18 MSG)

Who is the greatest teacher alive today? Pain. In the thick of the battle with our anxiety, we know that victory is on the way. Pain in this life—especially pain from anxiety—is inescapable, but suffering? Well, suffering is optional.

My struggle with anxiety develops my character and teaches me much-needed lessons that I cannot learn any other way.

Journaling Prompt

Certain much-needed personal lessons can only be learned through struggle. What lesson(s) has my struggle with anxiety taught me?

Prayer Time

Dear God, thank you for being present in all the junk of my life. Help me to remember that your never-ending grace has the power to promote a forceful change in my heart—change that molds me into an authentic human being, who values spiritual maturity over everything else. Amen.

#2

We must cling in faith to all we know to be true. For we have a magnificent King-Priest, Jesus Christ, the Son of God, who rose into the heavenly realm for us, and now sympathizes with us in our frailty. He understands humanity, for as a man, our magnificent King-Priest was tempted in every way just as we are, and conquered sin. So now we draw near freely and boldly to where grace is enthroned, to receive mercy's kiss and discover the grace we urgently need to strengthen us in our time of weakness.

HEBREWS 4:14–16 TPT

*I*n your journal or notebook, record your responses to the following questions for reflection:

- Over the past ten days, what three teachings have impacted me most?

- What is God telling me about how I cope with my anxiety?

- With that in mind, how can I improve how I cope with my anxiety?

- What actionable steps can I take to improve how I handle my anxiety?

More Gratitude

*He made us; we didn't make him. We're his people,
his well-tended sheep. Enter with the password:
"Thank you!" Make yourselves at home, talking praise.
Thank him. Worship him. For GOD is sheer beauty,
all-generous in love, loyal always and ever.*

PSALM 100:3–5 MSG

I become overwhelmed with anxiety on a daily basis. I become overwhelmed mainly with my responsibilities and the future. This is the thing though: my current responsibilities were at one time a prayerful wish for me. My career that I often feel burned out from? I prayed so many times that I would make it through grad school so that I could start a "real job." My kids who are now learning to navigate their own relationships, drive their own cars, and make their own decisions? I prayed so many times for a family when I was a kid; I've wanted to be a mom for as long as I can remember. I have that now.

Sometimes I look around at my anxiety-riddled life and hear an inner voice: *Isn't this what you wanted? Isn't this what you prayed you would have one day?* It turns out I have short-term memory issues. Nothing feels worse than a punch to the stomach than the reminder of how ungrateful I've been (okay, maybe that's an exaggeration. A lot of things feel worse than a punch to the stomach.).

My daughter, Brooklyn Grace, has the loveliest bedtime ritual. She keeps a coffee mug next to her bedside. Inside the coffee mug are popsicle sticks that she's decorated with colors, textures, and labels like "rode bikes with Dad," "started a new art project," or "Facetimed with best friend." Each night before bed, she begins to pull sticks out of her "happiness jar" and focuses on the good that happened in her life that day. With those grateful thoughts, she sleeps more soundly, and a restful sleep lends to a good day when she wakes up. I want to be like my daughter in this way.

I want to remember all the goodness God's given me each day instead of focusing on what I think I'm lacking. I want to aim my attention on beauty and grace instead of becoming bewitched by the negative stuff. Why do I waste what you give me? Why do I complain? Where is my gratitude, and why am I so easily forgetful of everything you've gifted to me?

You might be thinking, *Didn't we discuss gratitude already*? Yep. We read about the importance of gratitude back on day 7. We're talking about it again because it's that important. After all, there are over one hundred and thirty verses on thankfulness in the Bible. My husband sets alarms on his phone throughout the day, and when one of them sounds, he's reminded to speak the things for which he's grateful and pray. (In case you need a quick roadmap on how to pray, try the A.C.T.S. method: Adore, Confess, Thank, and Supplicate.)

A practice of gratitude will be sublimely helpful in our struggle with anxiety. Blotting out feelings of worry or sadness with reminders of progress and gratefulness may not always be our first instinct. But with practice and time, we can learn to respond to anxiety with openness and praise. Over time, I have even learned to be grateful for my anxiety. She points me in directions that I wouldn't have planned for myself.

The practice of gratitude is one of the most important ways to dissolve anxiety, and I must take its practice seriously.

Journaling Prompt

What are three things I can be grateful for today?
What are three things I was grateful for yesterday?

Prayer Time

*Father God, how many times can I say thank you?
It will never be enough. I get so easily wrapped
up in my daily discomforts and negative thoughts
that I forget how much you've come through for
me already. Please help me to remember each and
every way you take care of me. Amen.*

Power in Proximity

[Jesus] said to them, "My heart is overwhelmed and crushed with grief. It feels as though I'm dying. Stay here and keep watch with me." Then he walked a short distance away, and overcome with grief, he threw himself facedown on the ground and prayed.

MATTHEW 26:38, 39 TPT

One of the many, many attributes of Jesus that I find so captivating is that he was 100 percent God yet 100 percent human at the same time. One of the reasons I love the Gospels is that I have a chance to read firsthand how Jesus was every bit of a human as I am, with all of my very real human emotions of anxiety, sadness, and distress.

In this particular passage we are reading from today in the book of Matthew, Jesus knows what the night will bring: a betrayal and then an arrest. In his distress, Jesus asked his disciples for the gift of their proximity—to be near to him while he struggled under the weight of a certain future. Then he left them and prayed to his Father for guidance and peace. He prayed so hard in his anxiety and distress that Scripture tells us he was sweating bullets of blood.

I see several lessons in this particular passage of Scripture that I can apply to my personal battle with anxiety. There could be no clearer instruction based on the actions of Jesus in this verse. First, when we are feeling overwhelmed, weary, anxious, and fearful, we are to engage other loved ones in our battle because, surely, we cannot do this alone. Second, when we are feeling overwhelmed, weary, anxious and fearful, we are to *pray*.

We can achieve proximity to our Savior through prayer, but we should also seek proximity to our most trusted loved ones, as we see in these verses where Jesus is seeking comfort in the presence of his friends, Peter, Jacob, and John, and where Job has his circle of friends surrounding him also. There is power in proximity.

Honesty hour: Sometimes I get very bitter in the midst of what I perceive to be unfair life circumstances that cause my anxiety to flare up. My thoughts become something along the lines of, *Well, God, if you would just fix this, then it would be so much easier to be peaceful.*

When I think of biblical examples of sadness, grief, absolute unfair life circumstances, and every right to feel bitter, I think of Job. In the book of Job, we follow a man who seemed to be living life just as God asks us to: faithfully and blamelessly. Job is doing everything right, but then he loses literally everything in life that a person can hold dear: his wife, his children, his staff, his livestock, his livelihood, and his health. Job's response to all of the devastating loss is grief but also faith. He seems to understand (certainly better than I do) that pain in life is inevitable. He states to his wife, who in her own grief is hurting and angry with God, "'You're talking like an empty-headed fool. We take the good days from God—why not also the bad days?' Not once through all this did Job sin. He said nothing against God" (Job 2:10 MSG).

Next comes one of my favorite parts of the story. One day, in the thick of his grief, Job sits on the ground, covered in his own filth, because he doesn't know what to do. Along come his friends Eliphaz, Bildad, Zophar, and Elihu; they've heard the news of Job's losses, and they want to help. Let's read how they choose to help their friend:

> When they saw him from a distance, they could hardly recognize him; they began to weep aloud, and they tore

their robes and sprinkled dust on their heads. Then they sat on the ground with him for seven days and seven nights. No one said a word to him, because they saw how great his suffering was. (Job 2:12–13 NIV)

Job's friends see his pain, his hurt, and his suffering, and they choose to simply sit with him. His friends are not offering ideas on how Job can change his situation, explaining what got him into this mess, or suggesting what he could have done differently. They grieve with him in silence.

What's described here in this passage of Job is similar to the Jewish practice of *sitting Shiva*. When a person has lost someone beloved, other beloveds come near and support. When a beloved in our life has anxiety over an uncertain future, one of the best ways we can care for them is to simply offer our presence—not advice, not solutions—and be available.

When we feel overwhelmed with emotions, the last thing we should do is isolate. When we have a loved one who we know is struggling, the last thing we should do is leave them. Job needed his friends; Jesus needed his friends. We *all* need a person in our life that we can turn to when we are anxious and overwhelmed.

The closer I am to Jesus, the closer I am to peace.

Journaling Prompt

What is an example of a time when I allowed my anxiety to push others away from me? What was the end result of this isolation? What is one example of a time when I overcame my vulnerability and sought out the support of a loved one in the midst of my anxiety? What was the end result of this nearness?

Prayer Time

Dear God, thank you for the accessibility I have to you, the very source of my hope. When my fear is crippling, you're the peace. Help me to draw nearer to you every day in the knowledge that only by being closer to you do I have any hope of achieving peace. Without you, peace is not an option on the table. Amen.

Pray and Thank

*Don't fret or worry. Instead of worrying, pray. Let
petitions and praises shape your worries into prayers,
letting God know your concerns. Before you know it, a
sense of God's wholeness, everything coming together
for good, will come and settle you down. It's wonderful
what happens when Christ displaces worry at the center
of your life.*

PHILIPPIANS 4:6–7 MSG

I'm a firm believer in the mind-body-spirit connection. It is the
framework I use as a mental health provider, and with this mindset,
I often ask a new client about his or her spiritual beliefs as I try to
get to know them.

A few years ago, I had a new patient whom we'll call Marcy in
my office. I did not feel as though Marcy was given a fair chance
at life. Her rough upbringing and abuse history led to a turbulent
adulthood, and she was now a single mom dealing with heaps of
legitimate fear on a daily basis. She was badly struggling for a lot
of reasons, one of which was her meager support system. Marcy
was lonely.

Marcy's grandfather was at one time a strong source of support, but he had passed about two years before Marcy's daughter
was born. Marcy recalled her grandfather's temperament in session
with me one day: gentle, patient, peaceful, and rarely flustered.

Marcy wondered if her grandfather was this way because of his faith in God since he had been a devout Catholic.

She had recently started to attend church herself, in hopes that she would feel loved, supported, and cared for. She hoped to find other gentle souls like her grandfather because she was beginning to understand how difficult it is to do life alone. Marcy even ended up joining a Bible study with several other young ladies. (This was completely out of her comfort zone; I was so proud of her for taking this initiative!)

One day in Bible study, Marcy revealed her struggle with anxiety. Sadly, she was not met with kind words but rather verses like Philippians 4:6 and Matthew 6:25, which seemed accusatory to her. Marcy decided not to return to that particular church and even questioned if God was angry with her for being anxious.

If you are someone who has ever experienced anxiety and turned to the Bible for answers, I am 100 percent certain that you've come across today's verse. I am also 100 percent sure that if anyone has ever made you feel as though your anxiety is a sin, then they used this verse to support that accusation.

Are the instructions from Paul here to literally never, ever worry? I'm doubtful. While an anxiety-free life is something that God surely wishes for us and is something worth striving for, an anxiety-free life is an unrealistic expectation since we are all born with an innate stress response system.

While I don't take Paul's words literally here, I see nuggets of wisdom in this verse. I see the emphasis Paul places on prayer and gratitude in the midst of our anxiety. God's greatest desire is that we would turn to him before the lies of our anxiety drown out his voice. When we feel anxious, we are instructed to pray. Not lament on Facebook. Not complain to our coworkers. Not numb ourselves in destructive ways. We are to go directly to the source of our hope through prayer.

It is also important to note in this verse that turning to God in prayer does not instantly relieve us of our angst. Does this piece of Scripture guarantee that once we pray, our anxiety is magically lifted away? Heck no! The verse tells us that we will have a *sense* of everything coming together for our good. And the way I interpret this is that *we* are the ones who are changed through prayer, not the circumstances or situation.

Here's another translation of this verse from Philippians. Take note of the emphases on prayer, gratitude, and relationship with God:

> Be cheerful with joyous celebration in every season of life. Let your joy overflow! And let gentleness be seen in every relationship, for our Lord is ever near. Don't be pulled in different directions or worried about a thing. Be saturated in prayer throughout each day, offering your faith-filled requests before God with overflowing gratitude. Tell him every detail of your life, then God's wonderful peace that transcends human understanding, will guard your heart and mind through Jesus Christ. (Philippians 4:4–7 TPT)

It's a simple-in-theory, hard-in-practice formula: every anxious thought that crosses my mind is a reminder to *pray* and *thank*. As I do these things, peace will eventually come. Any change in life takes practice, and as we practice, these efforts become easier.

When I am anxious, my intuition should lead me to pray and to thank.

Journaling Prompt

Have I ever been told that I am sinning because I feel anxious? How did that make me feel? Do I believe that I am sinning when I feel anxious?

Prayer Time

Father God, thank you for loving me enough to want this daily communication with me. Day after day, you seek me out. I still cannot understand why you would want little old me as your companion. Please help me to use my anxiety as a daily reminder to turn to you and the peace that you bring. Amen.

Reframing

Those who sow with tears will reap with songs of joy.
Those who go out weeping, carrying seed to sow, will
return with songs of joy, carrying sheaves with them.

PSALM 126:5–6 NIV

*I*t used to be that I would wonder why I have an anxiety disorder. I would ask God, *What good could this possibly be doing?*
What is your plan here? How much longer will it be like this?
Maybe you are doing everything right. You've seen the therapists,
you're taking the medications, you've made the lifestyle changes,
and still you struggle. You want to know *why,* but you also want to
know *when.* When will this all be over? When will you feel whole
and happy and peaceful?

How many times have you been on your knees, weeping for
relief from your anxiety? How many times have you started to lose
hope, wondering if it will always be this way? Knowing the *why* of
things can be really helpful in coping, but we can't always know
why. We can, however, rest assured that God can use our anxiety struggles for good. I love the determination of Joseph in this
passage of Scripture from Genesis 50:20: "You intended to harm
me, but God intended it for good to accomplish what is now being
done, the saving of many lives" (NIV).

I love to talk back to my anxiety like this: *You're trying to hurt*
me, but God's gonna turn this around for good somehow. It will
be worth it in the end. Sometimes we feel an emotion so strongly

that we think we will always feel that way. Friend, this is not true. Emotions lie to us sometimes, especially our anxiety. God promises us peace. Maybe not in the way we want or the timing that we want, but it will come one day.

Our Scripture reading today from Psalms talks about harvest time. We Christians love our metaphors, and *harvest time* is a metaphor that is used a lot. *Sowing and reaping* is a metaphor that's used a lot too. This concept of putting in the hard work now for something that won't pay off until far in the future can be applied to anxiety.

We can find beauty in waiting. We can find wisdom in waiting. When our prayer for healing is not immediately answered in the way that we want, it's also possible that our lack of healing is somehow, some way protecting us from something. If you've ever enjoyed the immense privilege and luxury of seeing a therapist (and if you ask me, everyone should see a therapist at some point in their life!), chances are you were exposed to a technique called Cognitive Behavioral Therapy (CBT).

CBT is great. The premise behind CBT is if you change the way you think, then you'll change the way you feel. A lot of reframing work happens in CBT to challenge any cognitive distortions you may have, some of which you may not even be aware. Our anxious thoughts may immediately ask, *Why is this happening to me?* But we can refocus and reframe by asking, *What is this teaching me? How is the situation or the stressor developing me? Am I praying for God to change my situation, or am I praying for God to change me?* The reality is that God is weaving a story that I cannot see right now. I can't possibly know how my personal struggle with anxiety will help others or what benefits the struggle will eventually bring me.

Moreover, Jesus calls us to live abundantly *now*—not when we are healed, not when we feel like we have a better handle on our circumstances and anxiety, not some nebulous day in the future, but *now*. We read these words of Jesus in the book of John: "A thief has only one thing in mind—he wants to steal, slaughter, and destroy. But I have come to give you everything in abundance, more than you expect—life in its fullness until you overflow!" (10:10 TPT).

We like to take shortcuts. God takes us along the backroads because he sees it all: our future, our peace, and our becoming. We must learn to reframe our anxiety over seemingly unanswered prayers in this way: *God, what are you protecting me from? God, what is your plan for me in this? God, how can I use this situation and this struggle to help others who are on a similar path? How can I enjoy my life, right now, in the midst of my anxiety battle?*

We can certainly use our anxiety as a directional tool that points us to the areas in our lives in which we are not living in fullness and in need of transformation. Let's consider how we fit into God's master plan rather than trying to conform his plan to ours.

**Strong emotions will attempt to fool me
into believing they are permanent,
but I will rest knowing that healing is coming for me.**

Journaling Prompt

What is one example of when I felt like God took too long to answer one of my prayers, especially a prayer for relief or healing from my anxiety? Did the healing eventually come? Did it come in the way or shape I wanted it to? Is it possible God was protecting me during the waiting?

Prayer Time

Dear God, thank you for being my safeguard. You have the ability to play the long game and to see ahead in ways I will never be able to. I am learning to trust you in the waiting. I know my healing will come one day. Amen.

Perseverance

Isn't it wonderful all the ways in which this distress has goaded you closer to God? You're more alive, more concerned, more sensitive, more reverent, more human, more passionate, more responsible. Looked at from any angle, you've come out of this with purity of heart.

2 Corinthians 7:11–13 msg

This may be the most obvious statement in the world that I am about to make: pain hurts. It's uncomfortable and raw and exhausting. It's only natural that as humans we would try to avoid pain at all costs. Chronic anxiety is painful, certainly. All the uncertainty adds up. It's heavy.

Do you believe me when I tell you that we serve a Savior who is familiar with pain? He loves us so much that he took our pain on himself. He is a man well-acquainted with sorrow. We read about his agony in Isaiah:

> Yet he was the one who carried our sicknesses
>   and endured the torment of our sufferings.
>   We viewed him as one who was being punished
>   for something he himself had done,
>   as one who was struck down by God and brought low.
> But it was because of our rebellious deeds
>   that he was pierced
>   and because of our sins that he was crushed.

He endured the punishment that made us completely whole,
and in his wounding we found our healing. (53:4–5 TPT)

When we go to Jesus with our struggles and cry out, "This really hurts. I'm in pain," we can trust that we are talking to someone who can honestly say, "I understand because I've been there." If we persevere through the pain, get comfortable with being uncomfortable, and follow the guidance in our verse today from 2 Corinthians to let our distress bring us closer to him, then we make ourselves available for something stunning. We see a great example in John of how pain can produce something beautiful:

When a woman gives birth, she has a hard time, there's no getting around it. But when the baby is born, there is joy in the birth. This new life in the world wipes out memory of the pain. The sadness you have right now is similar to that pain, but the coming joy is also similar. When I see you again, you'll be full of joy, and it will be a joy no one can rob from you. You'll no longer be so full of questions. (John 16:21–23 MSG)

It seems that God is far more interested in developing my character and integrity than eliminating my discomfort. All of these traits described above in our reading from 2 Corinthians? I want to be all of them: alive, sensitive, reverent, human, passionate, responsible, pure, near to God, in the way of salvation, and living a life without regrets. I want to learn how to be grateful for productive pain.

It took me a while to shift my thinking to this: the goal is not complete relief from anxiety; the goal is nearness to God. There is power in proximity, remember? As Psalm 34:18 reads, "If your heart is broken, you'll find GOD right there; if you're kicked in the gut, he'll help you catch your breath" (MSG). When we are hurting, he is there. Period.

It's easy to get stuck in a vicious cycle of avoidance, numbness, and control. When we allow our anxiety to separate us from God, it's disastrous. But when we catapult our anxiety and allow it to drive us closer to God, we reap so. Many. Benefits.

When I am close to pain, I am close to God.

Journaling Prompt

What is one example of when I chose to draw near to God in the midst of my anxiety? Did this help to soothe my anxiety? What reminders can I put into place to ensure that persevering in seeking God is my reflexive response when I am feeling overloaded with my anxious thoughts?

Prayer Time

Father God, thank you for wanting to be close to me. What a gift, that you would seek me out—me with all my flaws and failures. Help me to remember this secret formula: pain that drives me to you will spark a type of healing above and beyond what I think I need. You know best, you know best, you know best. Amen.

All Things New

*I am doing something brand new, something unheard of.
Even now it sprouts and grows and matures. Don't you
perceive it? I will make a way in the wilderness and open
up flowing streams in the desert.*

Isaiah 43:19 TPT

Another one of my favorite clients is someone we'll call Sam. Sam has been through the wringer. She suffered childhood abuse from her biological father and became a single mom at a young age. She's endured a string of incredibly stressful jobs and a workplace robbery, which worsened her post-traumatic stress. Despite all the hard work she is doing in her recovery, she feels like there is no room to breathe and no one to turn to.

She asks me often if she's too far gone, if it's hopeless for her, and if she's unfixable. She asks me this because the work of healing is hard, and the healing doesn't usually feel good when we're in the thick of it. At first, sometimes the healing feels like breaking. It's only once we reach the other side that we are glad for having made the journey. This is what I said to Sam and what I would say to you too: there is always, always hope. God is making all things *new*. He is working miracles beyond our ability to comprehend. Our small human minds can't grasp what he is capable of.

We read this in the book of Ephesians: "Never doubt God's mighty power to work in you and accomplish all this. He will achieve infinitely more than your greatest request, your most unbelievable dream, and exceed your wildest imagination! He will outdo them all, for his miraculous power constantly energizes you" (3:20 TPT). What would it look like to move through life with the assumption that your struggle is only temporary, that help is on the way? What would it look like to constantly be chained to hope?

We also can't forget this verse in Philippians (it's a Hall of Fame type of verse that even non-Christians have seen or heard, along with John 3:16 and Jeremiah 29:11): "I can do all this through him who gives me strength" (4:13 NIV). The *very same chapter* in the Bible that gives us this famous creed of "be anxious for nothing" (Philippians 4:6) also gives us the famous verse "I can do all this through him who gives me strength." We have all seen these verses crocheted on pillows at Grandma's house and painted on wooden signs at Hobby Lobby. The sequence of these verses is not a coincidence, friend. Christ knows what an Armageddon the mind can be. He's here to help and support us along our journey.

If we are serious about living out this new resurrection-life we have in Christ, we should show it through our actions. We have to show up and do the hard work. There is eternal, everlasting hope for all of us. You are not a lost cause just because you are dealing with chronic anxiety. He's never late. He's working all things out for you, in your favor, for your benefit. Please don't give up on him and don't give up on yourself.

Hope is real, and healing is possible.

Journaling Prompt

When is the last time I can recall feeling truly hopeless? What was the situation? How did I handle these feelings of hopelessness? Did my approach get me the results I wanted? How could things have worked out differently if I went in with an assumption of hope?

Prayer Time

Dear Father, thank you for your faithfulness to me. Please forgive me when I doubt you. Please send me reminders of hope, over and over, because I'm forgetful. I know you have my best interest in mind always. Amen.

Return to Prayer

> But there's also this, it's not too late—GOD's personal
> Message!—"Come back to me and really mean it! Come
> fasting and weeping, sorry for your sins!" Change your
> life, not just your clothes. Come back to GOD, your God.
> And here's why: God is kind and merciful. He takes a
> deep breath, puts up with a lot, this most patient God,
> extravagant in love, always ready to cancel catastrophe.
> Who knows? Maybe he'll do it now, maybe he'll turn
> around and show pity. Maybe, when all's said and done,
> there'll be blessings full and robust for your GOD!
>
> JOEL 2:12–14 MSG

Living in the suburbs of Cincinnati, we have many locally owned restaurants with one of a kind, mouth-watering entrees. We love our local Indian food restaurants, Peruvian food hangouts, and German food joints. And then another family favorite is of course Chick-fil-A.

Have you ever fasted from eating before? I have, and it's tough. Fasting has its roots in Old English and German language.[5] Essentially, fasting is to voluntarily go without eating for a set period of time. In a religious context, the goal of fasting is to take the time and energy that you would have put toward preparing and consuming food and redirect them into a religious practice, such as prayer. For a Christian, the discomfort that a person experiences during times of hunger can also be a reminder of the suffering that Christ experienced.

There are many examples in Scripture of the ritual of fasting alongside other actions and emotions. We see people in the Bible fasting out of praise (Judges 20:26), out of grief (1 Chronicles 10:12; 1 Kings 21:27), in the midst of pleading (Ezra 8:23; 2 Samuel 12:16), in the midst of confession (1 Samuel 7:6), and in the midst of a send-off into new adventures (Acts 13:2–4).

What if we approached anxiety the same way we approached the ritual of fasting? What if we reframe anxiety as a call to prayer? What if, much in the way we allow the hunger pangs during a time of fasting to prompt us to pray, we repurposed our day-to-day anxious thoughts as prompts for us to pray—to seek him, to approach him, to hold him above all else? He wants us to call out to him, friend. This is what Paul writes in the book of 1 Peter: "Pour out all your worries and stress upon him and leave them there, for he always tenderly cares for you (5:7 TPT).

With practice we can learn to suffocate anxious thoughts with prayer and return to God. We can return to his compassion, his grace, and his vast, specific, plenteous love for us. He wants us, friend. He wants our wreckage and our angst and our doubt and all of it. He will never, ever leave us no matter how messy it gets.

I understand that the topics of eating and food may be triggering for some people. If this is you, I want you to know you are in my heart as I write this, and I would love for you to seek out a therapist who can help you in this area.

As hunger pangs remind me that it's time to eat, my anxious thoughts remind me that it's time to pray.

Journaling Prompt

Have I ever undergone a ritual of fasting? What was that experience like? How can I shift into the habit of allowing my anxious thoughts to trigger prayer, much like the ritual of fasting triggers prayer?

Prayer Time

Dear God, thank you for creating me in such a way that nourishing ourselves can be so enjoyable. Thank you for a strong body, and help me to use my body and my mind in service to you and to stop the train of anxious thoughts by interrupting them with prayer. Amen.

No Casualties

*Be strong. Take courage. Don't be intimidated.
Don't give them a second thought because GOD, your
God, is striding ahead of you. He's right there with you.
He won't let you down; he won't leave you.*

DEUTERONOMY 31:6 MSG

It's only natural to turn to a loved one for comfort when you are hurting. It's only natural to feel more hurt if that loved one dismisses your anxiety with simplistic advice or minimizes your struggle. Have you experienced this? Maybe you've worked up the courage to be vulnerable with another person about your anxiety disorder, but you were met with one or more of the following responses: "but you don't look anxious; you have so much to be grateful for; you just need to pray more; other people have it worse than you."

It takes a lot of vulnerability to admit your anxious struggles to someone else, but then to have that loved one give such unhelpful advice can be very discouraging. While I know that people have good intentions and want to help soothe my worries, I sometimes feel like they want me to be calm so that they, in turn, can remain calm.

One of the most terrible pieces of advice you can ever give to someone who struggles with anxiety is "Oh, don't worry about it, everything will all work out!" Oh, right! Don't worry. That's brilliant advice. I hadn't thought about trying that yet. "Don't worry" is not only impossible, but it also unfortunately often has the opposite effect, causing me personally to focus even *more* on my worry.

We read in our Scripture text for today in the book of Deuteronomy about Joshua's worries going into battle. The unknown, the uncertainty, and the fear of failure are eating him up. He's so young, so inexperienced, and likely feels ill-equipped for this new assignment. Moses, in an effort to bolster his confidence, speaks words of encouragement to Joshua: be strong and courageous.

I can picture Joshua right now. Sweaty and grimy from the noonday sun. Perhaps fatigued from his body armor, weary from marching in the desert, eager for rest, but understands a battle must first be won. Trying to focus on the assignment ahead, all while acutely aware that all of Israel is watching this commissioning he's received from Moses (social anxiety, anyone?).

We actually read this phrase *four times* in the span of just a couple chapters: be strong and courageous. Moses knows Joshua is scared. He isn't asking Joshua to shake off his worries and anxieties but rather to be courageous *despite* his fear.

Recall on day 8 when we learned how it's possible to feel two conflicting emotions at the same time. We can feel fear *and* courage at once. We can feel anxious *and* hopeful at the same time. What would have happened if Joshua had said no to this undertaking? What if he had allowed his anxiety to stop him from what God had planned for him in Canaan? Most likely, he would have really, really missed out. Giving in to his anxiety would have caused him a lot of regret. This possibility reminds me of this verse in Luke:

> What I'm trying to do here is get you to relax, not be so preoccupied with *getting* so you can respond to God's *giving*. People who don't know God and the way he works fuss over these things, but you know both God and how he works. Steep yourself in God-reality, God-initiative, God-provisions. You'll find all your everyday human concerns will

be met. Don't be afraid of missing out. You're my dearest friends! The Father wants to give you the very kingdom itself. (12:29–32 MSG)

What an incredible statement and reminder to us in our personal battles with anxiety. *The Father wants to give us the very kingdom itself.* A wildness awaits us, and we do not want to miss out on the great things our Father has planned for us.

I will not allow the great things that God has planned for me to become casualties of my anxiety.

Journaling Prompt

What does my anxiety steal from me? What is an example of when I gave in to my anxiety and ended up regretting it later? What is one wild hope or dream that my anxiety is holding me back from achieving? What are three concrete action steps I can take in the next thirty days to achieve this goal?

Prayer Time

Dear God, thank you for your constant encouragement and focus in my life. Help me to get lost in the rhythm of you and to continually remember that you are the sole source of my courage and strength, especially in my battle against anxiety. Amen.

Seek God

> *"Because he loves me," says the L*ORD*, "I will rescue him;*
> *I will protect him, for he acknowledges my name. He will*
> *call on me, and I will answer him; I will be with him in*
> *trouble, I will deliver him and honor him. With long life I*
> *will satisfy him and show him my salvation."*
>
> PSALM 91:14–16 NIV

Remember in the very beginning of this book when we talked about using caution when reading about promises in the Bible? Our verses today from Psalms are some of those verses we should read carefully and with discernment. If we breeze through them too quickly or take a verse out of context, we may interpret these specific passages to mean that all we have to do is love the Lord (and exactly how would we do this?), and then we are entitled to anything we want from life. This way of thinking is dicey because *when* (not *if*) the contentment in life that we expect doesn't come, we may feel short-changed and lied to by God.

Our verses for today's reading are used by a lot of people to demand healing of anxiety from God, to essentially tell God that he owes us something. This verse can also be used to shame people who are not experiencing relief from their anxiety. *It says so plainly that the Lord will deliver anyone in trouble, so if he hasn't, then clearly I am doing something wrong, or I'm not worthy enough, right*? Wrong. The following verse from Psalm 37:4 is one of the big offenders in terms of making us think that we are doing something wrong. It convinces us that he's not healing us because we're not honoring him: "Take delight in the LORD, and he will give you the desires of your heart" (NIV).

I'll be the first to admit that I tend to focus only on the second half of this particular verse, which talks about me getting what I want, and I overlook the first part of this verse, which includes some instruction I need to follow. It's a lot more fun to focus on one day being healed from anxiety, but I don't always like to focus on the *work* that it may take to get there.

This version of Psalm 37:4 makes it a little more clear that the goal in life is not to get what we want but to become more Christ-like: "Find your delight and true pleasure in Yahweh, and he will give you what you desire the most" (TPT). By becoming more in tune with Christ's way of thinking, our very desires change and mold into those of our Savior. We need to remember this every time we feel trapped in our anxious thought patterns. What I used to desire most was complete and everlasting freedom from anxiety. What I now desire most is closeness with Christ. I know that this will be more beneficial for me in the long run.

As I shift my goal from achieving a worry-free life toward a life of seeking God, my heart-ambitions will change, and I will experience less anxiety as I become more in tune with God and his plans for me.

Journaling Prompt

What is one example of a time when I went after my own desire without considering what God's desire for me would have been? How did that work out?

Prayer Time

Father God, thank you for caring so much about me. Help me as I seek after you so hard that one day we will be on the same page about everything in life. I know that this closeness with you will in turn help to relieve my anxiety. Amen.

Healed, Not Cured

*In front of all the people, she blurted out her story—
why she touched him and how at that same moment
she was healed. Jesus said, "Daughter, you took a risk
trusting me, and now you're healed and whole. Live well,
live blessed!"*

LUKE 8:47–48 MSG

ealed and whole. That particular word pairing is music to my
ears. Today, as we read about the healing of the woman in Luke 8,
is a good day to talk about healing versus curing. What comes to
mind when you hear the word *healing*? What do you mean when
you use the word *cured*? In my mind, these two words are often
used interchangeably but have very different connotations.

Curing is the complete removal of symptoms or an illness, as if
it never existed in the first place. For example, you get strep throat,
and you start on penicillin. The infection goes away, and you never
deal with the symptoms again. This to me is curing. Anxiety and
depression do not have a cure, but a person can be healed from
their struggles.

Healing, however, is very different from curing. Healing is
not necessarily the absence of symptoms but the restoration of
the whole person—mind, body, and spirit—along with peace and
acceptance of an outcome. A person can be living with cancer but
experience healing in their spirit. A person can say, "It is well with
my soul," when all is not well with their body. It's also important to

understand that healing is not the linear process that most of us expect it to be. It is often two steps forward, one step back, or two steps forward, three steps back. It can be tough to tackle but so worth it in the end.

I have one particular patient (let's call her AJ) who I have been working with for several years. She has been dealing with her anxiety disorder since she was a teenager. Her trauma and abuse history has left her feeling helpless, hopeless, overwhelmed, and out of control. Her all-consuming anxiety has led her to try to control her life in the ways that she can, like with her eating patterns. AJ has been waiting for *decades* for the healing to come. She's weary and beat-up. She's desperate for relief. She reminds me of the woman in Luke 8.

We don't know her exact name, but we read about the woman in Luke 8 who has been suffering for years from her affliction. Her illness is described as being physical (an "issue of blood" some of the older versions of the Bible tell us). Even though her illness is not mental, there is no difference between physical and mental illness. For instance, diabetes and depression are equally weighted and equally worthy of treatment and consideration.

We read that the woman in Luke 8 has been to many physicians, and no one has been able to help her. She has invested a great deal of time and money with nothing to show for it. She hears that Jesus is in town, and she's heard that Jesus is a healer. She becomes singularly focused on one thing: getting close enough to Jesus that she can touch him and be healed.

The text for this particular woman's story uses the word *healed* instead of *cured*. This particular woman's story has a happy ending. Not all stories in real life do. How long have you been waiting for healing from your anxiety? Weeks, months, years? I know that you, like AJ and like the woman in Luke 8, may be feeling hopeless and ready to give up your fight.

Healing is hard work, and healing often comes along with some discomfort because change is hard. Please don't give up. There is hope and there is healing. The healing may not come in the time frame that you want it to, but it will come. In the meantime, your job is to be persistent, keep the faith, reach out to Jesus, and be obedient to whatever he has for you. God is very, very interested in my becoming whole. Good grace, good God.

My struggle today is not indicative of my future healing.

Journaling Prompt

How long have I been waiting for my healing from my anxiety? Have I grown hopeless, believing that it may never come? How can I remain faithful in the waiting? How can I make healing my goal instead of curing?

Prayer Time

Father God, thank you for loving us so much that you will never leave us, even in the midst of our darkest days and our deepest struggles. Help me to hold on to this truth: you have good things ahead for me. Amen.

#3

*The way you counsel me makes me praise you more,
for your whispers in the night give me wisdom, showing
me what to do next. Because I set you, Yahweh, always
close to me, my confidence will never be weakened, for
I experience your wraparound presence every moment.*

PSALM 16:7–8 TPT

*I*n your journal or notebook, record your responses to the following questions for reflection:

- Over the past ten days, what three teachings have impacted me most?

- What is God telling me about how I cope with my anxiety?

- With that in mind, how can I improve how I cope with my anxiety?

- What actionable steps can I take to improve how I handle my anxiety?

Confirmation Bias

It stands to reason, doesn't it, that if the alive-and-present God who raised Jesus from the dead moves into your life, he'll do the same thing in you that he did in Jesus, bringing you alive to himself? When God lives and breathes in you (and he does, as surely as he did in Jesus), you are delivered from that dead life. With his Spirit living in you, your body will be as alive as Christ's!

ROMANS 8:10–11 MSG

*M*any years ago I was preparing to vote in a controversial presidential election. I won't say who the candidates were or who I voted for, but I remember that the candidate I was planning to vote for seemed like a no-brainer—qualified, confident, and on point with my values. All of the newspaper articles, all of the television interviews, all of the debates, and all of my friends on social media agreed with my opinion that my chosen candidate was clearly the best person for the job.

Looking back, I realize that I was falling prey to the psychological phenomena of confirmation bias. Are you familiar with this concept? It's a psychological phenomenon and cognitive bias in which a person has the tendency to search for, interpret, favor, or recall information in a way that affirms a prior belief. Confirmation bias affects virtually *all* of our attempts to interpret and understand the world and the people in it.

Let's break this down a bit. Before making a decision or forming an opinion, you would think that we as humans would carefully gather, examine, and consider evidence, and then we'd make a logical conclusion based on that evidence. However, this is often not what happens. It seems that we form an opinion or decision about something and then look for evidence to support it. This is confirmation bias. When I was preparing to vote for the next president, any positive information about my candidate was more likely to stick with me because I had already decided that they were ideal. This way of thinking is especially problematic when it comes to how we handle our anxiety.

Are you anxious about getting fired? Then you're more likely to interpret your annual performance evaluation as negative. Are you anxious about your kid failing ninth grade? Then you're more likely to construe their teacher's comments as hypercritical. What are your core beliefs about yourself when it comes to your struggle with anxiety? What if you've already decided that you will forever be an anxious person, that anxiety is your identity, and that anxiety will be something you always struggle with? Then your brain will go looking for evidence to back up your decision, to confirm this lie that you've already decided is the truth. Throw in some negative self-talk, like we read about on day 6, and this is a recipe for disaster!

The good news here is that you can reverse this cycle of negative thinking (or stinkin' thinkin' as my dad might call it). It takes practice and time, but it is possible to challenge your own belief system that you've built—a belief system that supports and even encourages you to be more anxious. When you only look for what you expect, you miss out on the surprising and unexpected, and you may not even realize it! One way to check your bias is to check in with a trusted and healthy person in your life and ask them to help you examine the facts. Chances are that this person will be able to approach the issue more objectively.

Look for the right evidence. There's room for reconciliation here. What you believe about yourself or about the world may not be the truth, so stop living like it is. Check the facts. Fight fear by replacing it with truth. Disprove your way of thinking negatively about yourself by hanging on to the words of God's truth.

Anxiety will fade when objective truth becomes front and center.

Journaling Prompt

What is an example of when I allowed confirmation bias to hijack my anxious thoughts? Was I able to recognize it in the moment? If yes, how did I handle this? If no, how can I do better next time?

Prayer Time

Dear God, thank you for being our ultimate Truth. The world may try to bring us down, but we know that we were not created for this world. Help me to overrule my own anxious thoughts by checking the facts of your truth. Amen.

Avoidance

*Beloved friends, what should be our proper response
to God's marvelous mercies? To surrender yourselves
to God to be his sacred, living sacrifices. And live in
holiness, experiencing all that delights his heart. For
this becomes your genuine expression of worship. Stop
imitating the ideals and opinions of the culture around
you, but be inwardly transformed by the Holy Spirit
through a total reformation of how you think. This will
empower you to discern God's will as you live a beautiful
life, satisfying and perfect in his eyes.*

ROMANS 12:1–2 TPT

The knee-jerk response to anxiety is sometimes avoidance, right? Pain is difficult and uncomfortable (remember reading about this on day 20?). Staying with the pain and fighting takes a lot of energy and endurance. It's easiest to leave or abandon our source of anxiety. We may skip class, stay home from work, stay home from the social event, or procrastinate the challenging task. Avoidance is the instinctual thing to do and usually gets us the immediate results or relief we are craving. We don't have to deal with the uncomfortable symptoms like a racing heart, sweating, feeling overwhelmed, or feeling that heaviness in our gut.

In mental health treatment, we talk a lot about avoiding triggers. Uncomfortable symptoms can be controlled in the short term at least by avoiding events or people that produced the anxiety in the first place. And while that's an appropriate recommendation in certain anxiety disorders—for example, a trauma-related stress disorder—avoidance over time does more harm than good for someone with more generalized anxiety. Because if avoidance is the only coping skill we ever learn, anxiety just worsens over time, eventually leaving us weakened and defenseless. Over time, avoidance just teaches our brain to fear harder.

In the past, and if I'm honest even still today, I've used avoidance as a coping skill. Usually it's when my social anxiety is acting up. It's much easier to decline an invitation to a party or pretend to have a sick kid at the last minute. This is worth repeating: Avoidance only brings short-term relief from the anxiety. Symptoms of anxiety will lessen, but it is only temporary. Long-term, the fear that initially led to the avoidance worsens since our brain learns that when the anxiety producing situation is avoided the symptoms go away. So, what do we do?

The verses in our reading today from Romans 12 tell us we should surrender and live in holiness, bucking the traditional ways of doing things, for the purpose of our own life-transformation, in response to the Lord's love for us. Instead of avoiding, we should surrender. This is easier said than done. Surrendering anxious thoughts to God? That is not usually my first instinct. Usually my first reaction is to listen to my panic. She's just so loud and strong sometimes. I'm learning that the loudest distractions in my life have run out of ideas on how to attract me. So, they resort to being loud.

This is what I know to be true:

- When I'm lost and insecure, God finds me.

- When I'm in over my head, he rescues me.

- When I am feeling overwhelmed, I can remember how he fights for me.

Even in the deepest pits of my anxiety, I can learn to find and name God's marvelous mercies and submit myself to him, which will, in turn, enable me to be transformed into the best version of myself by becoming more aligned with who *he* says I should be.

When it comes to managing my anxiety, I need to avoid avoidance.

Journaling Prompt

What is an example of a time in the past when I've used avoidance as my main coping skill? By using the tool of avoidance, did I get the results I wanted? Did I end up feeling anxious about other things as a result of my avoidance? Did I have any regrets?

Prayer Time

Dear God, thank you for loving me through my doubts, my avoidances, and my escaping. I will always be grateful for your patience with me as I learn. Help me to seek you and avoid my gut reaction of avoidance when it's not helpful for me long-term. When I run, help me to run in your direction. Amen.

Radical Acceptance

*We look at this Son and see the God who cannot be
seen. We look at this Son and see God's original purpose
in everything created. For everything, absolutely
everything, above and below, visible and invisible, rank
after rank after rank of angels—everything got started
in him and finds its purpose in him. He was there before
any of it came into existence and holds it all together
right up to this moment.*

COLOSSIANS 1:15–17 MSG

Okay, friends. Here's the ugly truth when it comes to anxiety: The expectation that we could live a life completely free from anxiety is not realistic. We will feel anxious at times. This is a fact. We are humans. We are not robots. As humans, we are emotions wrapped up in skin. We don't get the bodies without the feelings. It's a package deal. Since anxiety is a natural, often unavoidable response to certain stressors or situations, the goal should not be complete eradication of our anxiety. If this is the goal, then we're setting ourselves up for failure.

Management of our anxiety should be our goal. Remission of symptoms should be our goal. We have emotions, and learning to control and manage those emotions should be our ultimate objective. Spending the time to learn how to manage our emotions spares us from a countless number of poor choices or emotion-driven behaviors.

Here's another piece of ugly truth: sometimes we have to do the scary things in life while we feel afraid. If you wait until your anxiety is completely gone before you start to live your life, you will miss out on so much. Push yourself and do the scary things while you're still afraid to demonstrate to yourself that you are indeed capable.

There's a coping skill we teach in Dialectical Behavioral Therapy (DBT) called radical acceptance. Radical acceptance is not about just allowing dysfunction to run rampant around me. Acceptance does not equal approval. Acceptance does lead to problem-solving. Radical acceptance is about acknowledging reality and setting out on a hard-nosed path of coping. For some of us, we may have to radically accept that anxiety may be a part of our lives forever, much like Paul's thorn in the flesh that we read about in 2 Corinthians 12:7–8: "Because of the extravagance of those revelations, and so I wouldn't get a big head, I was given the gift of a handicap to keep me in constant touch with my limitations. Satan's angel did his best to get me down; what he in fact did was push me to my knees" (MSG).

We don't know exactly what Paul's limitation was; Scripture isn't specific on this. What we do know is that Paul struggled intimately and chronically with some sort of obstacle and was tormented by it. He prayed for relief. Satan even tried to use this to separate Paul from God, but Paul decided to use his struggle to drive himself closer to God. We can make the same choice.

There is no such thing as an easy, cushy life. You have to choose your hard. You can't have change and comfort simultaneously. Growth does not fall in your lap. Growth takes work. You have to actually *work* in your recovery. Healing does not come overnight. Healing does not come easily or passively or without a great deal of effort. But when the healing is complete, all the discomfort it took to get to that point is so, so worth it. I can truly attest to this.

Where we are weak, he is strong. When we feel empty, he replenishes. When we feel broken, he renews. When we feel the pressure coming from all directions and we feel closed-in, he is steadfast and immovable and will fight for us. His grace and his power will always be *enough*. Our unsteady and wobbly attempts will one day be used as evidence of life-transformation once God is through with us. He loves to show off the beauty and success of his children.

Our minds may tell us we're not good enough for him to be on our side. This is a lie. Our mind may tell us that we're not making progress quickly enough. This is a lie too. Any step in the right direction is valuable. Progress is progress. As my father so often says, "You're not where you want to be, but you're not where you used to be either." So, let's honor the space in between "no longer" and "not yet" when it comes to our personal recovery from anxiety.

Anxiety is a chronic struggle for most of us. Relief takes hard work, practice, and training. Believing that God is in control, which I absolutely believe, and knowing that he will work everything out for my good, which I absolutely know, does not free us from the responsibility of still working toward our goal. Let's give ourselves some grace in the process.

Anxiety may always be part of my story, but I can learn to manage my emotions while God uses this part of my story for my good and the good of the kingdom.

Journaling Prompt

What is the ugly truth that I can accept about my anxiety? What are two ways I can manage my emotions better? Am I willing to accept that my anxiety may always be a part of me?

Prayer Time

Father God, thank you for loving me through my anxiety. Help me to understand that the plan and future you have for me is best, even though I may not be able to make sense of it, now or ever. You know my future because you are my future. Amen.

Becoming Christlike

Jesus replied, "Now you finally believe in me. And the time has come when you will all be scattered, and each one of you will go your own way, leaving me alone! Yet I am never alone, for the Father is always with me. And everything I've taught you is so that the peace which is in me will be in you and will give you great confidence as you rest in me. For in this unbelieving world you will experience trouble and sorrows, but you must be courageous, for I have conquered the world!"

JOHN 16:31–33 TPT

During times of suffering, we want to know why. I have patients who ask me all the time why they continue to struggle and suffer from their anxiety disorder, year after year, with the same trip-ups. I'd like to offer a few concepts to you in order to help you reframe anxiety and understand the possible *whys*.

We are not promised an anxiety-free, safe, and comfy life as Christians. Scripture is pretty clear on the fact that there will be suffering and that suffering from any source—like our anxious thoughts—enables a believer to identify with the suffering of Christ and produces perseverance, character, and hope. There are some lessons that my stubborn self just won't learn any other way except through the Red Sea of my anxiety.

Pain and struggle are woven into the fabric of nature, *including us*. Year after year, the caterpillars undergo a miraculous metamorphosis that is both messy and uncomfortable but also rewarding and beautiful once they emerge as butterflies. Our agony can be reframed as something that helps us become more Christlike. That should be our daily goal, right?

Our suffering *from* and ultimate survival *of* a struggle with anxiety can be preparation for helping someone else who will go through the same thing we did someday. There's another *you* out there who needs to know that it's possible to survive this. Let's reframe our battle with anxiety as a way to lead and guide others on their own journey to healing.

Scripture also tells us that the reason behind our suffering is so that God can be magnified in the healing. There's an example of Jesus healing a man born blind in John 9 where the disciples asked Jesus why a man was afflicted with such a handicap. They want to know the *why* behind his suffering. Actually, it seems the disciples wanted to know who to blame. Jesus said neither the man nor his parents sinned. In other words, it was no fault of the man or his parents, but this affliction, this suffering, happened so that the works of God might be displayed through the man's healing. Our eventual healing from anxiety could act as a conduit for displaying God's power.

We can also reframe anxiety as a tool that Satan uses to separate us from God—or at the very least to get us to doubt him and ignore him. I've seen this to be true in my own life. I get derailed with my habit of overthinking and playing out every possible endgame. I try to control my way into assurance. I get fixated on the details, and the devil's in the details. I don't pray first, even though cognitively I know I should, because Satan's a master distractor. The more I think about this, the more fired up I get. How dare anyone try to come between me and my Savior? Satan really has some pluck.

We know that anxiety and fear can be some of Satan's most effective tools because of what we read in 2 Timothy 1:7: "For God will never give you the spirit of fear, but the Holy Spirit who gives you mighty power, love, and self-control" (TPT). That crushing feeling of doom about the future? Those intrusive, self-deprecating thoughts? Those are not from God, friend. God gives us a spirit of power and love. Anything else we know is from the devil, and he must be crushed.

There's no doubt that our anxiety can serve to separate us from Christ. All the more reason to break up with our anxiety. We can talk back to our anxiety and to the one who uses it as a weapon against us:

> Let God work his will in you. Yell a loud *no* to the Devil and watch him make himself scarce. Say a quiet *yes* to God and he'll be there in no time. Quit dabbling in sin. Purify your inner life. Quit playing the field. Hit bottom, and cry your eyes out. The fun and games are over. Get serious, really serious. Get down on your knees before the Master; it's the only way you'll get on your feet. (James 4:7–10 MSG)

Why do I have any hope of achieving peace? Because of him: "Because of you, Lord, I will lie down in peace and sleep comes at once, for no matter what happens, I will live unafraid!" (Psalm 4:8 TPT). Remember, God wants to be in relationship with us. Sometimes he may let us struggle so that we humble ourselves and turn to him. Let's make a pact to trust him more than we trust our fear.

When I feel as though I am suffering, I will rest in the knowledge that I am becoming more Christlike and growing as a Jesus follower.

Journaling Prompt

Of all of the reasons *why* discussed in today's
reading, which one resonates the most with me?
How can I use this new insight to reframe how I think
about my suffering from anxiety?

Prayer Time

*Dear God, thank you for the ultimate sacrifice that
could only have been achieved through suffering.
I forget so easily what you've given me; help me to
daily remember. You silence the fear. Help me to
change my perception of suffering and to reframe it
within the context of your love. Amen.*

History

I bless GOD every chance I get;
my lungs expand with his praise.
I live and breathe GOD;
if things aren't going well, hear this and be happy:
Join me in spreading the news;
together let's get the word out.
GOD met me more than halfway,
he freed me from my anxious fears.
Look at him; give him your warmest smile.
Never hide your feelings from him.
When I was desperate, I called out,
and GOD got me out of a tight spot.

PSALM 34:1–6 MSG

My personal anxiety lies consist of a lot of catastrophic thinking and trying to predict everything that could go wrong. If I can
predict, then I can plan and avert. I can prepare myself emotionally
for what may go wrong, instead of being blindsided. Logical, right?
Sometimes I think my tendency toward catastrophic thinking is
protective, like when my family is packing for a camping trip. We
wouldn't want to be stuck in the middle of the woods unprepared
for whatever nature throws at us, so my doomsday thinking is helpful in a situation like this. But my doomsday thinking is not helpful
when I'm looking in the eyes of my twelve-year-old child, who
happens to be a heart-stopping beauty, imagining all the terrible

things that could happen to her when she grows up and moves onto a college campus one day.

When my catastrophic thinking starts to kick off, I have to punt it off the rails before it gets too far down the track. How do I do this? I remember the history. Anxiety directs my attention to an illusion all the time. Fear makes fiction feel like fact. How can I counteract this? By looking at some cold, hard evidence. I force myself to recall and remember all the times my worst thoughts and fears did not come true. I try to remember all the prayers in my life that have been answered rather than focusing on the ones that haven't. I must remember all the times when I imagined the worst, and none of it happened. I must remember all the times everything worked out in my favor, by the grace of God, because his hand *is in everything*. I remember all the times I did survive a particular situation or circumstance to remind myself that I'll survive this time around too.

What I want more than just about anything when it comes to my battle with anxiety is *freedom* and to then use that freedom to serve others, like we read about in Galatians 5:13:

> God has called us to live a life of freedom. But don't view this wonderful freedom as an excuse to set up a base of operations in the natural realm. Constantly love each other and be committed to serve one another. (TPT)

I have a hard time seeing the good and the positive in anxiety-provoking situations. I can easily forget the history of my survival from anxiety. I want to do better at remembering. One of my secret weapons to help with this is writing down the good stuff. I forget so easily, and I really need those visual reminders. Possibly, this could work for you, too, friend. It doesn't have to be anything fancy or formal. Maybe a quick note in the margin of your Bible or a positive post on Facebook or a check-in on your mood diary app.

Bottom line: We don't want to lead lives full of what-ifs, focusing on everything that could go wrong. We can experience the freedom living that Galatians talks about and make ourselves more emotionally available to pour out love on those around us.

**In order to stop living a life of what-ifs,
I have to aim for the bullseye of truth and fact.**

Journaling Prompt

What are two recent examples of when I imagined the worst-case scenario? What was the result of that situation? Did my worst fear come true? How can I free myself up to love others?

Prayer Time

Dear God, I am so short-sighted sometimes. Strengthen my memory so I can easily recall the times I've survived. I know those times exist, but I'm so easily forgetful. Thank you for your ever-present help. All I have to do is ask, and you're there. Amen.

DAY 36

All of the Information

The fruit produced by the Holy Spirit within you is divine love in all its varied expressions: joy that overflows, peace that subdues, patience that endures, kindness in action, a life full of virtue, faith that prevails, gentleness of heart, and strength of spirit. Never set the law above these qualities, for they are meant to be limitless.

GALATIANS 5:22–23 TPT

I don't know how many of you, dear readers, have kids—or even how old they might be—but I myself am newish to the stage of raising teenagers. If you don't already know this, I'll clue you in: teenagers can be moody. So, on any given day, when my kid comes home from school and he's melancholy or irritable and doesn't want to engage in any sort of conversation with me, my anxiety kicks into gear, and I immediately start thinking something like this: *He's on drugs. He's being bullied. He hates me. I'm a terrible mother.* The reality is that I don't have all the information. Any number of things could be going on in my kid's life. Rather than catastrophizing about the worst possible outcome, what I need to realize is that I can't possibly have all the information right now.

This is my newest anthem and one of my favorite ways to combat anxiety. When I'm starting to get overwhelmed with my anxious thoughts, I tell myself: "I don't have all the information here." Telling myself this is super helpful in so many situations. When I'm feeling anxious. When I'm feeling critical. When I'm feeling judgy or judged. When I'm asking myself, *what if* ? When I'm feeling scared. When I'm playing the comparison game.

I can't know it all. It's just not possible to understand all the facets of a situation and what is inside someone else's head and all the influencing factors and the other forces at play. Life has layers. It's complicated sometimes. "I don't have all the information here" keeps me curious. This statement kicks off a fact-finding mission because surely there's an explanation other than the one I'm piecing together, a conclusion other than the one I'm jumping to. "I don't have all the information here" may even lead to a conversation with a person and, ultimately, empathy and connection.

What I do know is that an uninformed, preconceived notion, my own dang ignorance, only serves to harden my heart. I don't want to be hardhearted. I want to be a better thinker and feeler. I want to be selfless and open. This is one way I'm trying to get there: "I don't have all the information here." In the story I mentioned above about my moody teenage son, I used this tactic, and after I went on my fact-finding mission, it turned out he was a bit cantankerous because he was hungry. Well, that's a problem I can fix!

It's easy to fear what we don't understand. We can use this concept to improve our communication with others as well, which will in turn improve our anxiety. We can say to others, "Right now, I'm making up this story that…" and then fill in the blank with our anxiety lie.[6] This is a vulnerable practice, but when we use this statement, it gives the people around us the chance to correct our anxious illusions with reality.

Also, if we give him that chance, God can correct the lies that we believe about ourselves and the world around us. I may see more of the fruits of the Spirit evidenced in my thoughts and behaviors. I just might see more of the qualities I read in Galatians in myself. Why wouldn't I want to have a more patient, kind, and gentle response to the ones I love?

God loves us so much. He wants what is best for us, in a parental way. If we seek him, he can help us sort fact from fiction. He can help us understand what is truth and what is a lie from the pit of hell. This is how we fight our battles: we choke fear by replacing it with truth.

**When a situation brings me anxiety,
I must remember that I may not have all the information.**

Journaling Prompt

What is an example of a story or situation from the past week to which I didn't know all the pieces? Did I try to fill in the gaps myself, without getting any additional information first? How did that go for me? How can I do things differently next time?

Prayer Time

Dear God, thank you for your Spirit and divine love. Through it all, you are my constant and my reward and the good in my life. Help me to look back and never forget how you rescued me. Amen.

Celebrating Hope

*Our faith in Jesus transfers God's righteousness to us
and he now declares us flawless in his eyes. This means
we can now enjoy true and lasting peace with God, all
because of what our Lord Jesus, the Anointed One,
has done for us. Our faith guarantees us permanent
access into this marvelous kindness that has given us a
perfect relationship with God. What incredible joy bursts
forth within us as we keep on celebrating our hope of
experiencing God's glory!*

ROMANS 5:1–2 TPT

Trigger warning: this particular devotion mentions childhood
sexual abuse and cutting (a form of self-harm). I realize that some
of you reading this may not realize that cutting exists as a way of
coping for some people. Please feel free to skip today's reading if
this topic makes you feel unsafe.

I've been treating one particular patient for five years now.
Let's call her Toni. Toni survived horrific abuse from her family of
origin. After her biological sister and father died, she experienced
mental, physical, and emotional torture from her stepbrother and
stepmother, who eventually ended up selling Toni to a man who
worked in the industry of child slavery.

It's completely understandable that Toni has severe and overwhelming day-to-day anxiety. She's scared every day. She's trying
to make good decisions and get her life back on track, but some

days are really hard. Some days the pain is too much, so she cuts her skin superficially. Self-harm in this way and others, such as burning, skin-picking, and hair-pulling, are not healthy. I understand that Toni is not necessarily trying to kill herself; she's just trying to find a way to discharge the staggering, all-consuming pain in her heart. We all find our own ways to unload the pain of our anxiety.

Because of Toni's disquieting history, I have no logical reason that leads me to believe she will get better or recover or that her life will become easier. In a similar way, it's tough to believe that someone who has sustained such physical damage to their body will survive. How can a person even begin to move past such abuse? Please don't compare your story to Toni's and shame yourself into believing that you're not allowed to struggle because your trauma or the source of your anxiety looks different than Toni's. We all have our own hang-ups, and God cares for each and every one of us.

Professionally, I know not much else can be done for Toni. She's run the gamut of treatment options. If I were to tell her this, my fear is that she would decide life isn't worth living anymore, and she would do something to end it. Faithfully, I know that nothing is impossible with my God and that Toni has the potential to experience miraculous life-change.

But what if the relief doesn't come in this lifetime? What if the relief doesn't come in the timing we are hoping for? Will we remain loyal to him anyway, like the story of these brave men, recorded in the book of Daniel, who are presented with an ultimatum: die or worship another god?

Shadrach, Meshach, and Abednego answered King Nebuchadnezzar, "Your threat means nothing to us. If you throw us in the fire, the God we serve can rescue us from your roaring furnace and anything else you might cook up, O king. But *even if he doesn't*, it wouldn't make a bit of difference, O king. We still wouldn't serve your gods or worship the gold statue you set up." (3:16–18 MSG, emphasis added)

Will we have the fortitude and maturity to tell our anxiety, "I know God is going to rescue me, but *even if he doesn't*, I still trust him"? I hope so. I encourage Toni not to give up in her fight with anxiety. This is what I tell her, and this is what I would tell you: "Please don't give up. Please don't leave. This night won't last. Our God is a God of provision. He's our Jehovah Shalom. He's unstoppable. Not for a single second has he forgotten you."

God is rewriting our stories. He makes beautiful, beautiful things out of *dust*. He can surely take the mess of our lives and our struggle with anxiety and turn them into something dazzling. But even if he doesn't, I'm still with him.

Even though my healing from anxiety seems a long way off, I can still celebrate and focus on the hope that I have.

Journaling Prompt

If I'm being honest, where am I putting my hope? In whom am I putting my hope? How can I do the work of restoring my sense of hope in my future?

Prayer Time

Dear God, thank you for your eternal offer of hope and truth and life. When there's nothing good in me, you're the good. Fix my eyes on you. You remind me who I am, and you remind me that this pain won't last. Help me in the waiting. Amen.

Building a Balanced Life

*You realize, don't you, that you are the temple of
God, and God himself is present in you? No one
will get by with vandalizing God's temple, you can
be sure of that. God's temple is sacred—and you,
remember, are the temple.*

1 CORINTHIANS 3:16–17 MSG

I saw a patient in my office last week for a follow-up. We'll call
her Casey. On my first appointment with Casey, she was really
down. In the past two years, she suffered a stillborn death, the loss
of her career, and a home invasion. Because of all these traumatic
experiences, she found herself depressed and anxious. She had
trouble getting out of bed. She lost a tremendous amount of
weight because she stopped eating for a while. She had tried to
get help from different mental health providers, but she received
zero support from her family when she tried to get professional
help for her symptoms. They told her that since she was a Christian,
she should simply pray more and believe more, and then she would
be healed. Needless to say, this wasn't helpful advice for Casey, so
we worked together on other ways she could cope with her overwhelming emotions.

One day, she bounded into my office with great news: she was feeling like a million bucks. Not in a euphoric way but in a peaceful way. How did Casey turn things around? Her secret was self-care and the use of the DBT coping skill P.L.E.A.S.E.:

- **P & L**: Physical Illness (treat)

- **E**ating: (balance)

- **A**ltering drugs: (avoid mood altering drugs)

- **S**leep: (balance)

- **E**xercise: (get)

Self-care is a very trendy topic these days, right? Millions of results pop up if you perform a Google search on the best methods of self-care. We absolutely should care for our physical bodies by eating well, getting enough sleep, moving our bodies on a daily basis, and treating any comorbid physical illnesses. We learn in our verse today from 1 Corinthians that our very bodies are places of worship because God lives within us. This should prompt us to take care of our temples. God demands we take care of his creation, and this includes *ourselves*. We even see several examples of Jesus in the New Testament encouraging his followers to rest, sleep, and eat. Jesus himself often retreated from crowds to find moments of solitude.

We should also learn to care for ourselves so that we in turn can care for others. The two biggest commandments in all of Scripture are to love God and love others. You can't pour from an empty cup. You have to take care of yourself. There's a stark example in the Bible of the havoc wrought by lack of adequate self-care with a prophet named Elijah. He found himself desperate to the point of asking God to take his life:

When Elijah saw how things were, he ran for dear life to Beersheba, far in the south of Judah. He left his young servant there and then went on into the desert another day's journey. He came to a lone broom bush and collapsed in its shade, wanting in the worst way to be done with it all—to just die: "Enough of this, GOD! Take my life—I'm ready to join my ancestors in the grave!" Exhausted, he fell asleep under the lone broom bush. (1 Kings 19:3–5 MSG)

As the story continues, angels come to bring Elijah water and freshly baked bread. He then falls asleep for several hours. When he wakes up, he feels refreshed, energized, and motivated to the point of walking for the next forty days and nights to a particular holy place called Horeb. But the ritual of self-care can be a tough line to straddle.

Unfortunately, what I see happening in practice is that people use the excuse of self-care to shirk their responsibilities. Please let me reiterate this and please hear my heart: Self-care is not an excuse to shy away from or procrastinate your responsibilities or to behave recklessly. Doing something that makes you feel good in the moment (like a spending spree) but later stresses you out (as would an overdrawn bank account) is not true self-care.

I would like to propose to you that the ultimate form of self-care is creating a life that we don't need a break from. We must stop glorifying busyness and wearing our frazzled demeanor as a badge of honor. We must set healthy boundaries with our time. We must learn to declutter and rebalance. We can pray for the peace of God, but if there's no room to store that peace, it won't stick.

The greatest act of self-care is to build a life from which I do not need a break.

Journaling Prompt

What are two of my go-to forms of self-care? Are these rituals true self-care? How can I add self-care rituals like consistent exercise, good nutrition, and restorative sleep to my routine?

Prayer Time

Dear God, thank you for the gift of my physical body. My body may not look or feel how I want it to, but I know it's a gift to get out of bed every day. Help me to make good choices in how I care for myself. Amen.

Medication

*Jesus spat on the ground and made some clay with his
saliva. Then he anointed the blind man's eyes with the
clay. And he said to the blind man, "Now go and wash
the clay from your eyes in the ritual pool of Siloam." So
he went and washed his face and as he came back, he
could see for the first time in his life!*

JOHN 9:6–7 TPT

My patients who are Christians often ask me, "Is it okay for
me to take medication for my anxiety?" As Christians, some of us
hesitate to take medications. If we do, then that must mean we are
not relying fully on God for healing, right? Sadly, many Christians
are told or made to feel that taking medication is evidence of
weakness or a lack of faith on their part. This quote from The Grace
Alliance is spot on:

> Within many Christian circles, this topic [of taking antidepres-
> sants and similar medications for emotional or mental pain]
> comes with a lot of embarrassment and guilt. Why? Because
> when it comes to our hearts and minds, we hear an under-
> lying message that says, "Jesus is enough for all your needs
> (hearts and minds)." It comes across as if our emotional and
> mental pains are just spiritual problems…With this "Jesus is
> enough" perspective, I've heard countless stories of loving
> and well-meaning Christian leaders counseling others to

avoid or stop taking medications and simply trust God for mental and emotional healing.[7]

The idea that people are pressured to avoid or to stop taking a medication that has the potential to help them in their fight against anxiety brings me deep sadness. Yes, it is okay for a Christian to take medication for anxiety. Medication is one of the many tools God has provided to us to combat anxiety. Recall our reading from today's Bible passage in John 9 where Jesus heals the blind man by spitting onto the ground and forming a muddy paste, which he then placed on the blind man's eyes to heal him. Did Jesus need to use mud to heal this man? No. He could have commanded that the man be healed, but he didn't. He used a tool. And friend, when it comes to combating anxiety, medication is one of the many tools inside our toolbox. Utilizing this tool does not make you any weaker than a person who chooses to use other tools.

The decision to take medication for mental health is a deeply personal one, and there's a lot to consider. If you are considering taking medication as part of your treatment plan, then you'll want to know a few things. There are no magic pills, but meds can and do help a lot of people control their anxiety. I like to use the metaphor of cleaning a messy desk. Imagine that you are back in high school. You have a big term paper due the next day, and you've procrastinated until the last minute. Envision yourself sitting down at your desk to start writing this paper, and you realize your workspace is trashed: food, garbage, and junk everywhere. You realize that you will never be able to be productive in this type of environment. You need a bit of an overhaul in order to get your work done, right? Well, imagine if you had a helper.

Medication can be your helper. Medication can clean your messy desk so that you can get your term paper done. The meds don't write your term paper for you; you still have to do the hard work! But the meds help clear your head and boost your symptom control to a certain degree so that you feel more empowered and confident to get your work done. Make sense?

Here's another thing to remember: happiness and joy cannot be found in a tablet. Happiness and joy can only come from Christ. Medication cannot replace healthy self-care and good decision-making. If your anxiety is related to taking poor care of your physical body, a tiny pill will not overcome this. Medication can be helpful for numbing uncomfortable emotions, but sometimes it numbs emotions that you *do* want to feel. Sometimes it's appropriate to cry, and you want to cry, but medication can numb this response.

It often takes a bit of trial and error to find the right medication for you. Any relief a medication brings you needs to be worth the trade-off for the side-effects you experience. I always tell my patients that medication can help get you to the ballpark of where you'd like to be with your symptom control, but then your coping skills need to carry you the rest of the way.

Taking medication for anxiety does not make me less of a Christian.

Journaling Prompt

Is taking medication for my anxiety the next step in my recovery? What may be holding me back from taking this step?

Prayer Time

Dear God, thank you for loving me through all my struggles and trials. Help me to be able to discern if taking medication is the next logical step in my recovery from anxiety. Help me lean on you throughout the entire process. Amen.

Become a Source of Support

> *Love is large and incredibly patient. Love is gentle and consistently kind to all. It refuses to be jealous when blessing comes to someone else. Love does not brag about one's achievements nor inflate its own importance. Love does not traffic in shame and disrespect, nor selfishly seek its own honor. Love is not easily irritated or quick to take offense. Love joyfully celebrates honesty and finds no delight in what is wrong. Love is a safe place of shelter, for it never stops believing the best for others. Love never takes failure as defeat, for it never gives up.*
>
> 1 Corinthians 13:4–7 tpt

Maybe you picked up this book not because you struggle with chronic anxiety personally but because you have a loved one who struggles, and you want to learn as much as you can in order to be able to better support them. If you are the individual who suffers from anxiety, feel free to share this entry with a loved one who wants to support you.

I know you want to help. You see this person in your life, and something's off. Something's changed. They are not themselves. You want to help without making things worse, but maybe you don't have the right words yet. You don't know how to bring up your observations and concerns.

My first piece of advice would be to check your motive. Are you helping to truly help *them*? Or is your motive to decrease your own discomfort somehow, to relieve the effect that *their* distress has on *you*? Take a moment to reflect on what true love is, based on 1 Corinthians 13, part of which we read in today's passage. More than anything, the people in your life need to know that you truly love them.

Here are a few things that I would encourage you *not* to say to a loved one struggling with anxiety or with any mental health issue:

- "But you don't *look* depressed or anxious." Anxiety, along with all mental health issues, is often invisible. We have to be careful how we judge someone's outside presentation. You cannot possibly know what is going on inside of someone else's head and heart just by looking at them.

- "But you have so much to be happy about." This type of phrasing tends to minimize the pain someone is going through. It's a guaranteed way to make sure they never open up to you again.

- "There are people who have it worse than you." Again, this is minimizing their pain.

- "I know exactly how you feel." This may be the case, but this sort of statement actually turns the attention to yourself. Hold space for this person who feels comfortable opening up to you. It takes courage to open up to someone about anxious struggles. Don't betray their trust.

- "All you need to do is just…(believe more, pray more, have more faith)." This is probably the quickest way to guarantee this person will never approach you again or feel comfortable coming to you with their pain.

Here are alternative statements you can say instead:

- I'm here for you.

- You are strong, and I believe in you.

- You are loved.

- Please don't give up. You are not alone.

- If you were not alive anymore, I would really miss you.

The last statement is particularly vital to say to someone who is struggling with suicidal thoughts. The lie of anxious depression is that "if I wasn't here anymore, it would be easier for people because I would no longer be a burden." This is a lie that needs to be corrected out loud and said face-to-face to the people we love to save them.

If you don't know the right thing to say, it's okay. Your presence alone can be soothing. It's okay to say nothing and just show up. Maybe show up with doughnuts.

I am capable of becoming a source of support to the loved ones in my life who struggle with anxiety.

Journaling Prompt

Who do I know in my life who seems to be struggling with anxiety? How can I tangibly help them this week? What words will I use to help them understand I care for them?

Prayer Time

Dear God, thank you for the loved ones you've put in my life. Help me to be sensitive to their mental health needs, to recognize their anxious struggles, to say and do whatever most puts them at ease, and to rely on you through the whole process. Amen.

CHECK-IN

#4

I waited and waited and waited some more,
patiently, knowing God would come through for me.
Then, at last, he bent down and listened to my cry.
He stooped down to lift me out of danger
from the desolate pit I was in,
out of the muddy mess I had fallen into.
Now he's lifted me up into a firm, secure place
and steadied me while I walk along his ascending path.

PSALM 40:1–2 TPT

*I*n your journal or notebook, record your responses to the following questions for reflection:

- What three teachings throughout the book have impacted me most?

- How has my understanding of my anxiety changed compared to my first check-in?

- What is God telling me about how I cope with my anxiety?

- With that in mind, how can I improve how I cope with my anxiety?

- What actionable steps can I take to improve how I handle my anxiety?

Conclusion

We've made it to the end of the devotional, friends. At this point, you might be thinking, *I've heard a lot of this stuff before, Amanda. I thought I would learn something new.* Well, there's nothing new under the sun, and perhaps you have a self-discipline gap instead of a knowledge gap. Let's consider this passage from Romans 7:

> I'm a mystery to myself, for I want to do what is right, but end up doing what my moral instincts condemn. And if my behavior is not in line with my desire, my conscience still confirms the excellence of the law. And now I realize that it is no longer my true self doing it, but the unwelcome intruder of sin in my humanity. For I know that nothing good lives within the flesh of my fallen humanity. The longings to do what is right are within me, but willpower is not enough to accomplish it. My lofty desires to do what is good are dashed when I do the things I want to avoid. So if my behavior contradicts my desires to do good, I must conclude that it's not my true identity doing it, but the unwelcome intruder of sin hindering me from being who I really am. (vv. 15–20 TPT)

Can you relate to this passage? You know what you need to do but can't seem to follow through on it. Or perhaps you do the opposite of what you know is best for you. Well, this is where I want to discuss the topic of behavioral activation. This topic applies not only to anxiety but also to any situation that requires us to modify our behavior or reactions.

The Behavioral Activation Theory tells us, essentially, that feelings follow action, not the other way around. Behavioral activation teaches us that if we take baby steps toward a goal and complete the goal, then the good feelings come afterward. We can apply this concept to anxiety by taking baby steps toward our goal of conquering whatever anxiety-provoking situation we encounter, knowing that it may not feel good until after we've completed the action successfully. Feelings follow action.

My mom recently reminded me that when I was fifteen or sixteen years old, she took me to a cardiologist. I was experiencing mild chest pain and palpitations, and my pediatrician recommended that I see a specialist. They diagnosed me with an "innocent heart murmur" and asthma. I was given an inhaler, which I rarely used because my physical symptoms were self-limited, rendering the inhaler mostly useless. Looking back, I think it's quite likely that I was experiencing the somatic symptoms of anxiety. My guess is that back then no doctor really thought to ask me about my emotions or consider that my physical symptoms might be rooted in my mental health.

We've come a long way in mental health treatment. We still have a long way to go—especially in the Christian context. Friends, anxiety does not make you a bad Christian. It does not mean that God is angry with you or that your anxious thoughts and feelings are sins.

If you were sitting here with me at my kitchen table, I would lean across, grab your hand, and tell you earnestly face-to-face, eye-to-eye, how much you are beloved and treasured and chosen for greatness. You have resurrection power running through your veins, friend. You certainly possess the capacity to master your anxiety.

I hope the words in this book, these words from my heart, have been helpful for you in your recovery from anxiety. It is my greatest desire that you experience control over your day-to-day anxiety by relying on God's strength and promises as well as the strength you possess through his love for you. Because you are one of his children, you possess resurrection-type power, even if you haven't fully realized it yet. Because of Jesus' grace and sacrifice, you have the power of restoration and redemption.

> People with their minds set on you,
>   you keep completely whole,
> Steady on their feet,
>   because they keep at it and don't quit.
> Depend on GOD and keep at it
>   because in the LORD GOD you have a sure thing.
> (Isaiah 26:3–4 MSG)

Please don't give up on our Savior because you feel forgotten. He's closer than you think and near to the brokenhearted constantly (see Psalm 34:18). Please don't give up on yourself because you have struggled for so long with your anxious thoughts. Hope is real, friend. Hope is so, so close because our Jesus, our living hope, is all around us, every second of every day. He's in the midst of every battle, and we can count that battle as joy because of his nearness. Remember these wise words from Paul and consider how your anxiety has the ability to serve you, not scar you:

> At first I didn't think of it as a gift, and begged God to remove it. Three times I did that, and then he told me, "My grace is enough; it's all you need. My strength comes into its own in your weakness." Once I heard that, I was glad to let it happen. I quit focusing on the handicap and began appreciating the gift. It was a case of Christ's strength moving in on my weakness. Now I take limitations in stride, and with good cheer, these limitations that cut me down to size—abuse, accidents, opposition, bad breaks. I just let Christ take over! And so the weaker I get, the stronger I become. (2 Corinthians 12:8–10 MSG)

With God on your side, you are bigger than the struggle. His capacity and your obedience lead to absolute abundance. I'd like to leave you with these benedictions:

> Now may the Lord of peace Himself grant you His peace at all times and in every way [that peace and spiritual well-being that comes to those who walk with Him, regardless of life's circumstances]. The Lord be with you all. (2 Thessalonians 3:16 AMP)

> GOD, do it again—bring rains to our drought-stricken lives so those who planted their crops in despair will shout "Yes!" at the harvest, so those who went off with heavy hearts will come home laughing, with armloads of blessing. (Psalm 126:4–6 MSG)

Notes

[1] "Generalized Anxiety Disorder," *Diagnostic and Statistical Manual of Mental Disorders* (5th ed.), (Washington, DC: American Psychiatric Publishing, 2013), 222.

[2] "WHO urges more investments, services for mental health," World Health Organization, accessed November 13, 2020, https://www.who.int/mental_health/who_urges_investment/en/.

[3] Madhuleena Roy Chowdhury, "The Neuroscience of Gratitude and How It Affects Anxiety & Grief," PositivePsychology.com, January 9, 2020, https://positivepsychology.com/neuroscience-of-gratitude/.

[4] Addys Mayers, "10 Most Stressful Life Events," Thrive Global, May 4, 2018, https://thriveglobal.com/stories/10-most-stressful-life-events/.

[5] "Fast," Dictionary.com, accessed November 13, 2020, https://www.dictionary.com/browse/fasting.

[6] Drake Baer, "One of America's most beloved authors just told us her 'number one life hack' for lasting relationships," Business Insider, August 26, 2015, https://www.businessinsider.com/brene-browns-biggest-life-hack-is-a-simple-phrase-2015-8.

[7] "Is it ok for a Christian to take antidepressants?," Grace Alliance, July 9, 2019, https://mentalhealthgracealliance.org/christian-mental-health-and-mental-illness/is-it-ok-for-a-christian-to-take-antidepressants.

Acknowledgments

Dear Reader, as a pastor's wife, anxiety sufferer, and mental health professional, I've been living at the intersection of faith and mental health for more than eight years. I decided a while ago to do everything I can to help others who are in the middle of something I have personally survived. You are holding the product of that dream in your hands right now. Thank you for purchasing and thank you for reading.

My Joseph, it's been seventeen years now, babe. I remember our first apartment, which was home to a few cockroaches and smelled like stale Cheerios, but it was ours, and we were a family inside that apartment. You are my best friend, and every single day you amaze me with your insight and clarity into situations that muddle me. You always have the right words with the right spin and the right nuance. You keep me calm. You're my Xanax in human form. You make all the things better.

My kiddos, thank you for putting up with parents who were babies themselves when they started having babies. We learn from you every day and are endlessly proud of you.

My parents, thank you for your utmost support and love. Even though you destroyed my childhood dream of becoming a jockey, I think I've moved on and found my true life's purpose.

J and J, you are our best friends, you speak our love language of *Parks and Rec* quotes, and I can't think of any other people on the planet with whom we would rather take a trip to Mexico in the middle of COVID-19. Yes, that was a thing we did.

My church family, you are one of the reasons I write.

My colleagues and patients at the Lindner Center of HOPE, I learn so much, so deeply, from all of you.

Julie, Lauren, and BroadStreet Publishing, you were the first ones to say yes to my passion-dream of normalizing the discussion of mental health in the context of church. Thank you, thank you, thank you.

T.S., I'm 100 percent certain that you will never read this book, but you should know that your albums were the soundtrack to most of my writing sessions, and my lifelong goal will be to perfect the art of Taylor-Swifting my writing.

Dear God, your heart, my words, your artistry.

About the Author

Dr. Amanda Porter is an introvert and writer who is passionate about faith, hope, mental wellness, and recovery. As a nurse practitioner who specializes in Integrative Mental Health, Amanda diagnoses, treats, and prescribes medication to patients of all ages, of every diagnosis, and across all levels of care. She is board-certified in internal medicine, psychiatry/mental health, and addictions and practices at the nationally renowned Lindner Center of HOPE, a freestanding mental health center associated with the local academic medical center, the University of Cincinnati.

Amanda earned her PhD in Mind-Body Medicine from Saybrook University, where her dissertation studies examined the biological basis of depression. She lives in a suburb of Cincinnati, Ohio, with her husband, Joseph, who is a filmmaker and director at Whitewater Crossing Christian Church. Together, Amanda and Joseph have two kids, a boxer mix named Marley, and a COVID cat named Izzy.

Follow Amanda on Instagram @AmandaPorterNP or on her website, AmandaPorterNP.com.